ADDITIONAL BOOKS FROM PLANTING ROOTS

Flourish Wherever the Military Sends You

Kindle Direct Publishing (2019)

Bible Boot Camp for Military Women

American Bible Society with Planting Roots (2019)

Beyond Brave: Faith to Stand in Military Life

Kindle Direct Publishing (2018)

Free to Be Brave: Moments with God for Military Life

Kindle Direct Publishing (2018)

MORE RESOURCES FROM PLANTING ROOTS AUTHORS

Marriage Maintenance for Her: Tune Up After Time Apart

Liz Giertz, CreateSpace Independent Publishing Platform (2018)

Marriage Maintenance for Him: Tune Up After Time Apart

Liz Giertz, CreateSpace Independent Publishing Platform (2018)

When Marriage Gets Messy: Overcoming 10 Common Messes Married Couples Make

Liz Giertz, CreateSpace Independent Publishing Platform (2018)

Holy in the Moment: Simple Ways to Love God and Enjoy Your Life

Ginger Harrington, Abingdon Press (2018)

Journey of a Military Wife series:

Directed: Steps of Peace

Deployed: Steps of Hope

Devoted: Steps of Love

Dedicated: Steps of Faith

Brenda Pace, American Bible Society (2017)

Medals Above My Heart: The Rewards of Being a Military Wife

Brenda Pace and Carol McGlothlin, B & H Books (2004)

The One Year Yellow Ribbon Devotional: Take a Stand in Prayer for Our Nation and Those Who Serve

Brenda Pace and Carol McGlothlin, Tyndale House Publishers (2008)

Olive Drab POM-Poms

Kori Yates, Crossbooks (2011)

PRAISE FOR GROWING TOGETHER

"Planting Roots is a trusted partner in ministry to the Global Military Community. I am not surprised that they would pick the book of Hebrews for a six-week Bible study for military spouses. The book of Hebrews is known for its focus on the preeminence of Jesus Christ. As my wife Lydia and I learned as a career Navy couple, it takes the power of Christ to see a person through life in the military. I highly recommend this Bible study to anyone who longs to reflect Jesus in the military."

> Joe Ludwikowski, Captain, U.S. Navy (Ret)
> Executive Director, Military Ministry of CRU

"I was completely captivated by Melissa Hicks' six weeks bible study, *Growing Together: Strength to Persevere in Military Life*, based on the book of Hebrews. Raised in a military family, and married to a military man, I desperately needed this study to keep me focused on Christ, reminding me of the importance of being in community with others as I struggled with unknown circumstances. Melissa guides you through scripture each week as she parallels military life with applicable stories from the Bible. She challenges you to dig deeper into the meaning of Scripture, and then live it out in your daily life and in community with others. This study will change your life and perspective, refresh your soul, and deepen your understanding of who Jesus is to us today."

> Susan Miller, Founder of Just Moved
> Ministry and author of *After the Boxes are Unpacked*

Planting Roots is a vibrant ministry for women who live the military lifestyle. *Growing Together* is a fresh new Bible study applying concepts from the book of Hebrews to the challenges of the military community. Melissa Hicks has written an engaging new resource that encourages military women band together for friendship and spiritual growth.

> Ellie Kay, Co-Host of The Money Millhouse
> and Founder of Heroes at Home

"In my almost 40 years of pastoral ministry, I have studied the Book of Hebrews more than any other book of the New Testament. It is an often neglected rich well of Spiritual refreshment. I was therefore excited to learn that Planting Roots chose this epistle for their Growing Together Bible Study. The Growing Together study specifically targets Military Women, and does so effectively. This study will challenge women to deepen their walk in Christ, and to accurately apply the powerful Scriptural truths of the book of Hebrews to the challenges of Military life."

Arthur "Art" Pace, Chaplain (Colonel-retired), U.S. Army, national vice-president of Military Chaplains Association, vie president of Planting Roots Advisory Board, and co-author off *Engage Your Strengths 4.0.*

Growing Together: Strength to Persevere in Military Life

A SIX-WEEK BIBLE STUDY BASED ON HEBREWS

A Planting Roots Bible Study by Melissa Hicks

Published by Planting Roots Corporation,

P.O. Box 84, Leavenworth, Kansas 66048

Unless otherwise noted, all Scripture quotations are from The ESV® Bible (The Holy Bible, English Standard Version®), copyright © 2001 by Crossway, a publishing ministry of Good News Publishers. Used by permission. All rights reserved.

Written by Melissa Hicks

Cover design by Ginger Harrington

Cover Photo by Jacob Lund via Canva

Editorial Team: Ginger Harrington, Jennifer Wake, Andrea Plottner, Muriel Gregory

H2O concept is from DisciplesMade®

Graphics VectorStock® expanded license, Canva Free Media License

Planting Roots is a nonprofit organization encouraging military women to grow in their faith.

CONTENTS

INTRODUCTION

Without continual growth and progress, such words as improvement, achievement, and success have no meaning.
- *Benjamin Franklin*

It is called growing pain for a reason. Growth is painful, challenging, and even scary. Babies and children do not have a choice in the matter. They grow, change, and develop. It is a hectic time of both physical and intellectual growth. As an adult, we have a choice to stay stagnant or continue to grow intellectually and spiritually.

I have struggled to grow at times. Sometimes it was due to
- Busyness
- Distractions
- Lifestyle
- Isolation

The impermanence of the military lifestyle has often stunted my growth.

The truth is that as Christians, we do not have a choice. God loves us too much to leave us where we are. Fortunately, God has also provided a community in which I can blossom.

Those communities have been a place of
- Fellowship
- Accountability
- Forgiveness
- Grace

Wikipedia defines a community as a social unit with commonalities such as norms, religion, values, customs, or identity. Communities may share a sense of place situated in a given geographical area or virtual space through communication platforms.

I have found communities in Bible studies, book clubs, running groups, or directly in my neighborhood. Planting Roots has become a significant community for me.

Most conservative Christian scholars date Hebrews after the death of Paul (around 65 A.D.) and before the destruction of the Jerusalem temple (70 A.D.) The book of Hebrews encourages a community of believers struggling to persevere. Their world was dramatically changed as they faced persecution for their newfound beliefs.

Though written millennia ago, the truths, exhortations, and encouragement found in this book are very applicable to our transient lives.

Without community, I would have crumbled under
- Extended deployments
- Absence during the holiday season
- Passover for promotion
- Orders to a duty station I did not want
- Another casualty notification
- Parenting struggles

> *And let us consider how to stir up one another to love and good works, not neglecting to meet together as is the habit of some, but encouraging one another, and all the more as you see the Day drawing near. —Hebrews 10:24-25*

These verses will be our guiding light throughout this study.

To grow and persevere, we all need a strong foundation: Jesus. This is the starting point of our journey.

Identifying what stunts our growth is crucial. What is holding me back? What habits and beliefs do I need to overcome?

We are made for community. I need to be a source of encouragement and love to the people around me as much as I need their love and support.

Community is where we grow and persevere — the place where we blossom. Bloom where we are transplanted is a reality of the military lifestyle—and a source of growth.

This six-week study is topical. It is based on the book of Hebrews, but it also draws on other passages in the Bible. The daily homework will allow you to dig deeper into each topic studied. All you will need is this book, a Bible and a willingness to learn. Are you ready to journey with us and discover how we can grow together and persevere in community?

Let's go!

Muriel Gregory
Lansing KS January 2020

WEEK ONE
I Want to Be Like Jesus When I Grow Up

What do you want to be when you grow up?

When I was a little girl, people often asked me this question. My answers were pretty typical of a girl in the '90s: mommy, teacher, marine biologist (during my "love of dolphins" phase). Now as a mom, I hear people asking my kids the same question. I see back-to-school posts on social media with pictures of smiling kids in new outfits holding up signs with their likes and interests, and often, what they want to be when they grow up. It's fun to think about, to imagine the possibilities.

Growing up is a process, and we don't always become the person we wanted to be when we were in kindergarten.

I also hear friends tell other friends they want to be like them "when they grow up." It's a compliment for sure. It declares that we haven't arrived yet, but we see something in the other person we admire and wish to emulate.

Let's ask a better question

Instead of asking what we want to be when we grow up, perhaps we should ask ourselves who we want to be when we grow up.

Romans 8:28-29 says, "And we know that for those who love God all things work together for good, for those who are called according to his purpose. For those whom he foreknew he also predestined to be **conformed to the image of his Son,** in order that he might be the firstborn among many brothers" (emphasis added).

The first part of that verse might be familiar to you. It's often used to remind people that God is working good for them, even when life doesn't always *look* good. But sometimes we misunderstand God's definition of good. The second verse (verse 29) clarifies it a bit for us. God is making us more like his Son, Jesus. This is the good he is working out in our lives.

As we grow and mature, we begin to notice how hard life is. Growing up as a military kid, it didn't take me long to realize the struggles. Sometimes moving was an adventure. Other times I wanted to dig in my heels and never PCS again. Sometimes it was exciting when my dad went to unheard-of places and brought back rare souvenirs. Most of the time, I just wanted him to be home to tuck me in at night.

When life is hard, I'm tempted to forget about who I want to be. I struggle to focus on anything but the difficulty of my circumstances. The only way to persevere is to redirect my gaze.

2

Consider Jesus

Growing up, I had to remind myself that my dad wasn't just working a 9 to 5 job. He was serving our country. He was protecting me by serving in the military, and ultimately, that was for my good.

Spiritually speaking, growing up is no different. The harsh realities of our world threaten our endurance. But when we set our eyes on Jesus (Hebrews 12:2), we find comfort and the strength we need to mature and grow into the person God wants us to be, a reflection of his Son.

Knowing Jesus, understanding his character, and going beyond the basics are crucial elements for our spiritual growth.

This week, we're going to attempt to gain an accurate view of Jesus from the book of Hebrews. This will enable us to set our focus on Christ's strength and truth, even when life is complicated.

HOMEWORK

In your homework this week, we will draw from the Book of Hebrews and study what the author reveals about the character of Jesus.

And let us consider how to stir up one another to love and good works, not neglecting to meet together as is the habit of some, but encouraging one another, and all the more as you see the Day drawing near. —Hebrews 10:24-25

This week we will seek to stir up one another to love and good works by focusing on the character of Christ.

DAY 1: CONSIDER JESUS

The book of Hebrews was originally a letter written to a group of people who were struggling. They needed encouragement to hold fast to their faith and persevere in severe trials. Like us, military women faced with the realities of life and death, justice and injustice, they needed reminders that Jesus is Lord. They needed to hold fast to the truth that Jesus is better than anything else in which they might want to place their hope.

Much of Hebrews compares Jesus to Old Testament concepts such as angels, the law, Moses, priests, sacrifices, etc. The original readers were Jews who became Christians, forsaking Jewish customs and traditions to adopt a new life and lifestyle that come through faith in Christ.

They needed the reminder that Jesus is truly better than what they gave up. Armed with the knowledge of Christ's superiority, they can endure whatever comes their way. "Therefore, holy brothers, you who share in a heavenly calling, **consider Jesus**, the apostle and high priest of our confession" (Hebrews 3:1, emphasis added).

Considering Jesus, knowing who he is and what he does, is essential to growth and endurance. Below are some verses from the book of Hebrews that provide insight into who Jesus is.

1. Match the following verses with the character of Jesus:

Hebrews 1:3   Final and perfect sacrifice

Hebrews 1:11-12   High Priest who can sympathize

Hebrews 2:18   Exact picture of God

Hebrews 4:14-16   Eternal, unchanging

Hebrews 9:25-26   Helper to tempted people

These verses are a small representation of how Jesus reveals himself in the book of Hebrews. In reality, the entire Bible is about him. It is a life-worthy goal to never stop studying and reflecting on Jesus' character. Too often who we think Jesus is and who the Bible says Jesus is are very different things. Let's dig in a little more to see if we can develop a more accurate, Bible-based view of Christ.

2. Look again at Hebrews 1:3. Compare it with Colossians 1:15-17.

Verses	Jesus is	Jesus does	Jesus already did
Hebrews 1:3			
Colossians 1:15-17			

3. Jesus is God. He is powerful enough to hold the world together and take away our sins. How does knowing this encourage you or bring comfort when you are struggling?

4. Think of something hard in your life right now. Choose one of the characteristics from Hebrews 1 or Colossians 1:15-17. Ask God to show you this aspect of himself in your current circumstances.

DAY 2: JESUS AND THE ANGELS

Change is a constant in military life.

- Locations
- Friends
- Deployment/redeployment dates
- Uniforms
- PT standards

Due to the transient nature of military life, it is pointless to put our hope in the military. We need something steady and secure and that will last beyond our next duty station or deployment.

1. Read Hebrews 1:10-12. List what you learn about God. Note the contrast in verses 11-12.

God is immutable. He has always been and will always be. His character, his will, and his promises never change.

Before we move on, let's consider the context. Context is important. We gain a better understanding when we read the preceding verses. Yesterday I mentioned that the book of Hebrews links Jesus to many Old Testament concepts. The first chapter of Hebrews compares Jesus to angels. Jewish people viewed angels as God's messengers. The Hebrew word for *angels* (*ággelos*) means messenger, envoy, one who is sent.[1]

---

[1] https://www.blueletterbible.org/lang/lexicon/lexicon.cfm?Strongs=G32&t=KJV

2. Read Hebrews 1:7-8. List what you learn about angels. List what you learn about the Son (Jesus).

Angels	Jesus

Jesus is better than angels. He is not just a messenger of the good news that God has rescued his people. Jesus is both the messenger *and* the rescuer! Our eternal, unchanging God came down to earth as a man to rescue us. We can put our hope in him!

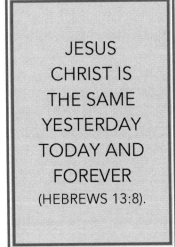

JESUS CHRIST IS THE SAME YESTERDAY TODAY AND FOREVER (HEBREWS 13:8).

3. What is currently changing in your life? How can God's immutability bring you comfort?

4. How can you put your hope in the unchanging God rather than your changing circumstances? List specific ways you can put your faith into action.

DAY 3: JESUS AND SUFFERING

Sometimes it seems like military life is synonymous with suffering. As military women, we undergo long periods of separation from our loved ones, a lack of support systems, misunderstanding from civilian counterparts, and high levels of stress. It is tempting to doubt the goodness of God, complain about issues, or attempt to control or change circumstances.

Jesus also lived a life of suffering. It was not only his last few days on earth that were a struggle. Coming to earth as a man, emptying himself of the glory he held in heaven, and dying for our sins are a few of the sacrifices Jesus made on our behalf.[2] His three years of ministry before his death were fraught with homelessness, transiency, rejection, ridicule, and ultimately an unjust death. To say that Jesus suffered is an understatement.

The very fact that he suffered and experienced temptation enables him to share in our pain.

1. For because he himself has suffered when tempted, he is able to help those who are being tempted (Hebrews 2:18).
Mark True (T) or False (F):

_____ Jesus suffered
_____ Jesus struggled with temptation
_____ Jesus doesn't understand
_____ Jesus can help me when I'm tempted

Don't forget our context here. The early part of Hebrews contrasts Jesus with angels (see Day One). Jesus is better because he chose to take on the human condition, unlike angels.

---

[2] Philippians 2:6-7

"The God of the Bible takes our misery and suffering so seriously that he was willing to take it on himself." -Timothy Keller[3]

I don't know about you, but this inspires me to trust Jesus even more. Write a short prayer of gratitude for what Jesus has accomplished in and for you.

2. How does understanding what someone is going through enable you to help?

3. How are you suffering right now? In what ways are you tempted?

4. What are some ways Jesus can help you when you struggle with temptation?

---

[3] https://www.facebook.com/TimKellerNYC/posts/2726642070708995

DAY 4: JESUS IS BETTER

"Jesus is better" is the overarching theme of Hebrews. Today and tomorrow, we're going to see how Jesus is a better High Priest.

1. Look up Hebrews 4:14-16 and write it below.

High Priest

Characteristics:.
* set apart men
* from the line of Aaron (Num. 3:10)

Duties:
* guarding the sanctuary (Num. 3:38)
* teaching (Deut 33:10)
* anointing kings (2 Kings 11:12)
* encouraging soldiers (Deut 20:1-4)
* supervising censuses (Num 26:1-2)
* making atonement for the sins of the nation (Lev 16)

This last piece – the atonement piece – is one of the most critical roles of the high priest.

Since Jesus walked on this earth, he can sympathize with us. He experienced temptation the same way we do. The difference was that Jesus did not sin. He did not have to make a sacrifice for himself as the high priests did (see insert about High Priest and atonement).

2. How does knowing that Jesus can sympathize with you encourage you? If you do not believe he can understand you, talk to him about it. Ask him to search your heart and show you where you are doubting. Ask him to reveal the truth to you.

3. Look up the definitions for *mercy* and *grace* and write them below. For *grace*, look for the Christian interpretation.[4]

Mercy –

Grace –

4. In what areas can you look to God for mercy and grace today?

Atonement

God instituted a system of animal sacrifice in which an animal would die, symbolically taking on the penalty of people's sins. With the death of the animal, the cost of the crime, and all the damage it caused would be paid (atonement). Jesus offers this atonement for us so that we can be made right with God. Knowing this, we can come to God with confidence, no longer fearing his judgment.

[4] https://www.dictionary.com/browse/grace?s=t

DAY 5: JESUS AS HIGH PRIEST

Have you ever had days when you couldn't get a straight answer from anyone? Like when you want to take leave, but the form has to be signed by three different people, two of which are on leave themselves and won't be back any time soon. Or it takes weeks for someone to come when you call housing to report a maintenance issue. They assess the situation, promising to send someone in a few hours to fix it. Instead, no one shows up. You're left with a leaking roof, sick kids, and a dog that pees all over the floor. Sometimes it would be nice to have someone who could fix our problems and give us a final answer.

Enter Jesus. Ok, so he's probably not going to come out and fix your roof or approve your leave, but he does offer us a final answer in a different, more crucial, eternal way.

1. Read Hebrews 9:24-28. This passage in Hebrews compares Jesus to another Old Testament concept (i.e., high priest), demonstrating that Jesus is better.

Contrast Jesus with the Old Testament High Priest.

High Priest	Jesus

Yesterday, we talked about animal sacrifices. It was a central part of the high priest's job – to make atonement for the people. Jesus, too, made a sacrifice. But not with an animal. He sacrificed himself. The high priests had to make sacrifices every year. Jesus only had to sacrifice himself once.

2. Look up Hebrews 10:11-13. What do you notice about the sacrifices the priests made? What makes Jesus's sacrifice so powerful?

In Hebrews 10:12, the phrase, *he sat down at the right hand of God* evokes both finality and kingship. This phrase is used throughout the Bible to show God's power and sovereignty.[5] Jesus has finished the work of salvation. He is sitting on his throne in heaven, and the payment for sin is complete. No one else needs to sacrifice. Jesus gives us the final answer to our most pressing problem. No, not the leave or housing issue—*our sin issue.*

Depending on what you're dealing with today, this might not feel like much. You want answers, solutions to the problems you're facing right now. I get it. There are days when I struggle to remember that Jesus solving my sin problem is the most important thing. But this is why we have spent the entire week considering Jesus. We need to remind ourselves that he is all he says he is and does all he says he will do.

We can trust him. And while we hear the drip, drip, drip from our ceiling, wondering when it's going to get fixed, we remember that this world is not our permanent home. We have a much better house waiting for us in heaven, one whose ceiling will never leak!

So let's depend on Jesus when life gets hard. Let's trust he is going to use these things for our good – not to make us happy or to give us a comfortable experience – but grow our faith and to transform us into the likeness of Christ.

3. Summarize the main ideas God has taught you this week. In what ways can you connect these biblical concepts to your everyday life?

---

[5] https://www.ligonier.org/learn/devotionals/seated-at-gods-right-hand/

H20: CONNECT WITH JESUS*

Draw near to God, and he will draw near to you. —James 4:8a

Reading the Bible is an essential habit for our everyday lives, especially as we strive to become more like Christ. It doesn't always happen organically. Intentionality is the key. If we want to consider Jesus as we have this week in our study, we need to connect with him daily.

Someone once told me that the Bible is how God communicates to us, and prayer is how we communicate back to him. As military women, we know that lack of communication creates a lack of intimacy. Talking and listening are vital components of a stable relationship. Below are three simple steps you can use to make reading the Bible an intentional, consistent part of your life.

- Look up a verse
- Read for context, the verses before and after, perhaps even the whole chapter.
- Journal your thoughts and questions. Possibly ask yourself, "What does this tell me about God? About other people? About myself?"

*H20 stands for Habits to Outcome. Each week we will introduce a particular spiritual discipline to help you grow and better apply the concepts of this Bible study.

DIGGING DEEPER: CONNECTING WITH HEROES OF THE FAITH

Did you know one of the Bible's greatest heroes was an assassin turned missionary? The Bible is filled with examples of flawed people who meet God in a variety of ways.

You might already know this story, but let's view it today with fresh insight. Acts 9 describes a story of transformation. It is a story full of drama, visions, and reluctant characters.

> But Saul, still breathing threats and murder against the disciples of the Lord, went to the high priest, and asked him for letters to the synagogues at Damascus, so that if he found any belonging to the Way, men or women, he might bring them bound to Jerusalem. Now as he went on his way, he approached Damascus, and suddenly a light from heaven shone around him. And falling to the ground, he heard a voice saying to him, "Saul, Saul, why are you persecuting me?" And he said, "Who are you, Lord?" And he said, "I am Jesus, whom you are persecuting. But rise and enter the city, and you will be told what you are to do. The men who were traveling with him stood speechless, hearing the voice but seeing no one. Saul rose from the ground, and although his eyes were opened, he saw nothing. So they led him by the hand and brought him into Damascus. And for three days he was without sight, and neither ate nor drank. —Acts 9:1-9

Dramatic, right?

Saul was an assassin taking down anyone who believed in Jesus. Through a strange turn of events, he met Jesus, lost his sight, and refused to eat or drink for three days. God then sent a man named Ananias – a believer – to go to Saul, pray for him, and restore his vision. Ananias was terrified. He knew Saul's reputation. Out of obedience, Ananias set out, not realizing the magnitude of what was about to happen.

> So Ananias departed and entered the house. And laying his hands on him he said, "Brother Saul, the Lord Jesus who appeared to you on the road by which you came has sent me so that you may regain your sight and be filled with the Holy Spirit." And immediately something like scales fell from his eyes, and he regained his sight. Then he rose and was baptized; and taking food, he was strengthened. For some days he was with the disciples at Damascus. And

immediately he proclaimed Jesus in the synagogues, saying, "He is the Son of God." And all who heard him were amazed and said, "Is not this the man who made havoc in Jerusalem of those who called upon this name? And has he not come here for this purpose, to bring them bound before the chief priests?" But Saul increased all the more in strength, and confounded the Jews who lived in Damascus by proving that Jesus was the Christ. —Acts 9:17-22

Meeting Jesus is life-changing.

Think about who you are now. Dream about who God wants you to be. Trust that the transformation will be remarkable

Consider Jesus, the apostle and high priest of our confession . . . .

Hebrews 3:1

WEEK TWO
Dangers of Drifting

The Army-Navy game is a long-standing rivalry within the military community. Every December, the two academy football teams face off in a battle for bragging rights. This 119-year tradition continues today, fostering friendly banter among branches and boosting the morale of the side that scores the most touchdowns. Beat Navy!

While I will cheer for Army until the day I die, I've also had to make some concessions to the Navy. For starters, they have a much greater understanding of a considerable part of our world – the water. As I researched nautical terminology for this chapter, I came across an interesting term that has some spiritual implications: "set and drift".

Set and Drift

Navy friends, humor me please. "Set and drift" is a term describing the "external forces that affect a boat and keep it from following an intended course." Both words are related to the effect of currents. Set refers to direction; drift relates to speed. "Ignoring set and drift can cause a mariner to get off their desired course, sometimes by hundreds of miles."[6]

In seeking to grow together and become more like Christ, we can sometimes veer off course. As we discussed in Week One, the book of Hebrews compares

---

[6] https://en.wikipedia.org/wiki/Set_and_drift

Jesus with many Old Testament concepts, proving that Jesus is better than angels, better than Moses, and he is the better high priest of a better covenant. The writer of Hebrews also intersperses warnings throughout the text to exhort us to hold fast to our faith. In Hebrews 2:1, we find the first warning. "Therefore we must pay much closer attention to what we have heard, lest we *drift* away from it" (emphasis added).

Drifting is a clear and present danger to our growth as Christians. It happens when our direction, or our speed of life, or both are off course. A subtle shift can cause a dramatic difference between our targeted destination and our actual port. In military life there are many causes of drifting:

- Busyness
- Moving
- Command climate
- Changes in season (i.e., marriage, motherhood, empty nest, new job)
- Rejection
- Loss
- Health changes (mental and physical)
- Sin

The Road to Maturity

How do we persevere no matter what is happening around us or inside us? The writer of Hebrews says, "We must pay closer attention to what we have heard" (2:1). What we have heard is that Jesus is better. He is the one in whom we can put our trust. How do we pay closer attention to Jesus in the demands of military life?

While it might sound simple, it is not easy. Military life is hard. Everything can be going well in one duty station. At the next one, you might feel like the rug has been pulled out from under you. You can excel under one commander and struggle to survive under the next one. Then slowly, often before we are even aware of it, we begin to drift. We start to doubt. We begin to harden our hearts.

To guard against drifting, we need to remember the gospel. Read it; study it; listen to it.

"The gospel says you are more simple and flawed than you ever dared to believe, yet you are more accepted and loved than you ever dared hope because Jesus lived and died in your place."[7]

Growing together with other Christians protects us from the danger of drifting. Let's keep our eyes open for people who remind us of Jesus. Intentionally pursue accountability and relationships that will help us stay on our desired course. The Christian life is not a solo life. We need others to point us back to Jesus.

The road to maturity requires us to fix our gaze on Jesus and guard against drifting. Don't walk it alone!

[7] Peter Scazzero, *The Emotionally Healthy Church* (Grand Rapids, Michigan: Zondervan, 2009), 83.

HOMEWORK

This week we will focus on some different ways we are prone to drifting and how we can prevent veering off course as we seek to "stir up one another."

And let us consider how to stir up one another to love and good works, not neglecting to meet together as is the habit of some, but encouraging one another, and all the more as you see the Day drawing near. —Hebrews 10: 24-25

DAY 1: NUMBING WITH DISTRACTIONS

There are times in my military experiences when I would prefer to feel numb. There's been too much pain. Too many goodbyes. Too much distance. I know what's coming, and I'd prefer not to feel.

Distraction is a tempting way to avoid pain and cope with the hard parts of military life. We all distract ourselves in different ways and for different reasons. We cram our calendars with activities, seek connections on a screen, escape into the fantasy world of entertainment. Sometimes we may even dull our senses with alcohol or drugs with desperate desires to numb pain and loss.

In what ways do you try to avoid the pain when you feel it inside? I get it. Numbing pain is a powerful temptation that can set us adrift. I wish we could sit down together and share the emotions and situations that are easier to avoid.

Sometimes distractions choose us. We have to eat; our kids can't sit in dirty diapers; the boss needs a response on that email; people are waiting for us to return their text or call.

There's a thought-provoking little booklet floating around called *The Tyranny of the Urgent.* In it, the author, Charles E. Hummel, discusses the tension we feel between important things and things that are urgent. He warns that our "greatest danger is letting the urgent things crowd out the important."[8]

Spiritually speaking, we need to be aware of what crowds out the things that are important to our growth as believers. We need to guard against our distractions.

---

[8] https://www.goodreads.com/work/quotes/7009749-tyranny-of-the-urgent

1. Read and paraphrase Ephesians 5:15-16.

We are all given twenty-four hours in a day. To use our time wisely, we have to decide what is essential and what is urgent. Remember that "set and drift" occur with all of us. Our pace of life and the direction we choose will impact our final destination.

2. What are some "set and drift" things in your life that keep you from staying on course in your walk with God? (Set refers to your speed; drift refers to your direction.)

Set (Direction)	Drift (Speed)
(Example: overscheduling)	(Example: scrolling social media instead of reading the Bible)

3. Look up Colossians 2:6-7. What does it mean to walk in Christ, "rooted and built up in him and established in the faith"?

4. How can you guard against distractions (both the ones you choose and the ones that choose you) so that you may continue to mature?

DAY 2: HARDENING THE HEART

When we drift in our relationship with God, becoming complacent or stagnant is another danger. It's easy to get carried away by our feelings, others' opinions, or self-rationalization of sin. These are a few of the hidden dynamics that can cause us to drift in faith. But there is an even greater danger. When the desires of our hearts drift from God, our hearts can eventually become hard. The author of Hebrews mentions this several times, referring to the stubborn, obstinate nature we develop.[9]

Sometimes our hearts harden when we experience one difficult experience after another, feeling like we can barely keep our heads above water before the next challenge pushes us down even farther. I experienced this during my husband's year-long deployment when a two-month extension came right at the end. Sometimes we harden our hearts because the one impossibly difficult situation we thought would never happen, happens. In the military, we face repeated losses that hit our communities hard. Sometimes our hearts become resistant when we sin repeatedly and refuse to repent.

Biblical Examples

Many people throughout the Bible struggled with difficult circumstances, distractions, and sin. Below are some passages you can look up to find out more.
Someone who struggled with one hard thing after the other: Naomi in Ruth 1-4 (esp. Ruth 1:1-5, 20-21). Read how God redeems her situation in Ruth 4:14-17.

Someone who was distracted: Martha (Luke 10:38-42)

Someone who sinned repeatedly without repentance: Solomon (1 Kings 11:1-10).

It is in the hard moments, the losses that barge into our lives, when we either draw closer to God or distance ourselves from him.

---

[9] https://www.blueletterbible.org/lang/lexicon/lexicon.cfm?Strongs=G4645&t=KJV

27

1. Read Hebrews 3:7-11 and describe what takes place.

Harden – to make hard, harden, to render obstinate, stubborn (https://www.blueletterbible.org/lang/lexicon/lexicon.cfm?Strongs=G4645&t=ESV)

Astray – deceive, err, go astray, wander, seduce, (https://www.blueletterbible.org/lang/lexicon/lexicon.cfm?Strongs=G4105&t=ESV)

In the verses above, the author of the book of Hebrews alludes to the time in which the Israelites wandered in the desert for forty years before they entered the Promised Land.

The Israelites saw how God provided for them in the wilderness. He fed them, clothed them, and protected them in miraculous ways. These are the "works" they saw (Hebrews 3:9), yet the Bible says, "They always go astray in their hearts; they have not known my ways." (Hebrews 3:10).

2. What happens when we see God's works, yet do not know his ways? Put another way, what happens when we see something God does but misunderstand his reasoning behind it?

When our hearts are hard, we cannot accurately understand what God is doing.[10] How many times do we see God work, but we doubt his goodness or his sovereignty? How often do we forget what God has already done? Could this be because our hearts are hard?

---

[10] https://www.gotquestions.org/hardened-heart.html

3. Read Ezekiel 36:26. Ask God to search your heart and reveal to you the areas that have turned to stone. Ask him to soften the callouses and to give you a heart of flesh.

DAY 3: THE RISK OF ISOLATION

Like I said earlier, I'm a bit of a Navy novice. However, I do know that to steer a large vessel in which the entire crew works together toward its intended port requires more than one sailor. Likewise, to live the Christian life and stay on course, we need other people. Living in community with other believers is one of the main ways we guard against drift.

I struggle to find a community within the military culture. Maybe you can relate. An introvert by nature, it's easy for me to isolate myself rather than continually build new relationships. And moving doesn't help. So often just when I've formed a few deep relationships, the orders come in, and it's time to go. After several moves, I've wanted to hold on to my old friendships, keeping up with them via phone or social media. Though not a bad thing, the fallout has been that I hesitate to fully invest in new connections.

I don't want to say goodbye to people I love...again.

But I've learned that virtual relationships are not the same as in-person friendships. Proverbs 27:10 says, "Better is a neighbor who is near than a brother who is far away." Neighbors see us regularly. They can tell when life is beating us down. They can also get to us much faster than our friend who lives across the country. We also need friends in the place where we are.

1. Read Ecclesiastes 4:9-12. In what ways are two better than one?

As military women, we need other believers to cheer us on, to remind us of what's true, to meet real needs (cover a shift, bring a meal, child or pet care, etc.). Without these relationships, we will drift. We will forget what God has done. We will get bogged down with the urgent things and neglect the important.

2. "Iron sharpens iron, and one man sharpens another" (Proverbs 27:17). What are some ways someone else has sharpened you spiritually? In what ways can you sharpen another believer? Why do you think this is important?

Accountability has practical value. Sometimes we need someone to check on us. One of my friends recently told me how she does this. She and her friend talk about their highs and lows and their buffalos. (The good, the bad, and the awkward). This simple phrase keeps them connected and is a great way to get beneath the surface of small talk.

I've taken my kids on play dates with other military Christian women who've asked me, "What's God teaching you right now?" Though that question often takes a few minutes to respond, it can open the door to a more in-depth, life-giving conversation than you would not have had otherwise.

We need others to hold us accountable; we all need women who encourage us to stay the course, to remind us how to be faithful to what God has called us to do. We also need friends to pray for us and to cheer us on when we cannot see what God is doing in our lives.

3. In the Old Testament, there's a story of a king who hunts down the prophet Elijah for betraying the king's military secrets. The king sends his entire army with horses and chariots to capture the prophet. Elijah's servant sees this and begins to fear. Elijah reassures him that they are safe because God sent horses and chariots of fire to protect them. Read 2 Kings 6:15-17. What does Elijah do for his servant? (v. 17)

4. Who in your life today needs you to pray like Elijah? Who can be an Elijah for you?

DAY 4: SPIRITUAL DRIFTING

When I was little, my family and I were on vacation at the beach. Unbeknownst to us, there was a rip current, and my brother was swept up by the powerful force. Though he was trying to swim back to shore, the current took him further and further out. My dad rushed to rescue him and was able to bring him back safely. When my brother came out of the water, he was very shaken up, as you would imagine. But he was also shocked to realize how far away the current carried him.

It's the same with spiritual drifting. Sometimes the current is subtle, but at times life can bring a riptide we didn't see coming. Caught in the current, we don't realize how far off course we've gone. Once we recognize our condition, we are faced with an important decision. Are we going to swim harder, fight the current, or cry out for rescue?

1. Luke 15:11-24 gives us a picture of someone who recognizes how far he's drifted. Look up the parable and record your responses below.

Who is drifting?	
How does he drift?	
What does he do when he realizes he has gone too far?	
Who rescues him?	

Notice that this is also a story of identity. The younger brother forgot who he was, forgot what his father had done for him. His need caused him to adopt a slave mentality. Embracing
his son with love, the father restores his identity as a son. Without lecture and without punishment, the father celebrates the son's return. This is a powerful illustration of the Father-love God extends to each of us!

When we come back to God in repentance, he waits with open arms to restore us.

2. Reread Luke 15:18, 21. How does the younger brother turn from his sin?

3. In what way was the younger brother prepared to swim harder? (i.e., to try harder, to work for his father's acceptance?)

4. Does God require you to swim harder, try harder, or work harder for love and acceptance? What do you think God expects from you?

Our God is like the father in this story. He does not want us to work our way back into his good graces by becoming a servant. All he looks for is a repentant heart, for us to turn our hearts to him.

When we drift, we can tell God we're sorry, admit that we strayed from him, and ask him to rescue us. He will bring us safely back to shore. He is a compassionate Father, standing ready with arms stretched wide, to welcome us back as children and celebrate our safe return.

> IF MY PEOPLE WHO ARE CALLED BY MY NAME HUMBLE THEMSELVES, AND PRAY AND SEEK MY FACE AND TURN FROM THEIR WICKED WAYS, THEN I WILL HEAR FROM HEAVEN AND WILL FORGIVE THEIR SIN AND HEAL THEIR LAND (2 CHRONICLES 7:14).

5. Are you drifting spiritually? Do you need to turn back to God and call out for rescue? If so, take a few minutes now and do it. Don't put it off. This is important. God waits to welcome you because he loves you more than you can possibly fathom.

DAY 5: JESUS AND US TOGETHER

Dog tags, military IDs, CAC cards, uniforms, insignia, ranks. We have many reminders of identity within the armed forces.

Our belief in Jesus gives us a new identity but with fewer outward symbols. While we may not wear a specific uniform, there is no doubt God is transforming us into a completely different person. Too often, though, we forget this. I believe this is another reason we drift. We forget who we are as God's deeply loved children. We identify more with the military or a particular lifestyle than with who God says we are.

1. Look up the following verses and fill out the chart below.

Verses	Description of Identity
John 1:12	
Romans 8:16	
Romans 8:17	
2 Corinthians 6:18	
1 John 3:1	

What do you notice as the common theme of our identity?

The Bible teaches that we are born slaves. We are enslaved to sin. But when we trust in Christ, God adopts us as his children, giving us all the rights and privileges that entails.

2. Imagine you were born a slave. Every day you performed manual labor. You didn't go to school or have time to play. There were days you didn't get enough to eat. Your clothes were old and worn. Then imagine that one day you woke up and were adopted by a loving father who provided for your every need. Your whole world changed. You wore designer clothes, ate the choicest of foods, attended the most prestigious school. How would you feel initially? Over time, what old ways of thinking or patterns of behavior might reappear?

As Christians, this is our reality. Similar to adopted children, we often revert (or drift) to our old thought patterns and behaviors. We forget who we are and whose we are.

3. What are some ways you can remind yourself of your identity as a believer? How would your thoughts and behaviors change if you daily believe you *really are* God's child?

H2O: JOURNALING*

Behold, I am doing a new thing; now it springs forth, do you not perceive it? I will make a way in the wilderness and rivers in the desert. —Isaiah 43:19

Connecting our Bible reading to our everyday life is an important habit for maturing in faith. Journaling provides a link between God's written word and our thoughts. It does not have to be complicated. Below are some simple steps to begin journaling:

- Read a passage of Scripture
- Write down a verse or two that stands out to you
- Paraphrase it in your own words
- Record what God is teaching you, either through the Bible or through your circumstances

We are busy, distracted people. Seeing one day at a time, we often miss the big picture of what God is doing. Journaling helps connect those dots. Over a few days, a week, a month, we can look back and trace the golden thread of God's hand working in our lives. A "spiritual about face" is an important faith-building maneuver for Christians. That is, turning around, looking back over our lives, and seeing what God has done.

*H2O stands for Habits to Outcome. Each week we will introduce a particular spiritual discipline to help you grow and better apply the concepts of this Bible study.

DIGGING DEEPER: CONNECTING WITH HEROES OF FAITH

Naomi was a woman who experienced significant losses. It started with a move, though not military-related. Her relocation was due to a famine. Sometime afterward, she lost her husband. Followed by the death of her two adult sons.

> *Now Naomi was in a foreign country, widowed, and grieving the loss of not just her husband, but her two sons as well. She decided to return to her home when word spread that the famine was over. She urged her daughters-in-law to return to their families of origin, but Ruth firmly decided to stay with Naomi. When they re-entered Bethlehem (Naomi's hometown), the people were surprised to see her. They asked, "Is this Naomi?" She responded, "Do not call me Naomi; call me Mara, for the Almighty has dealt very bitterly with me. I went away full, and the LORD has brought me back empty. Why call me Naomi, when the LORD has testified against me and the Almighty has brought calamity on me?"—Ruth 1:19-21*

Naomi experienced one hard thing after another. As military women, we can probably relate. While our stories might differ, experiences of loss, transitions, and hardship connect us. Naomi struggled. She grieved. She was angry with God. And sometimes we struggle with grief, bitterness, and resentment as well. The things Naomi thought would never happen, happened. Her life did not turn out the way she thought it would. It wasn't supposed to be this way. Maybe you can relate on some level…

But God.

Those two powerful words can transform a person's story from loss to life. That is precisely what happens in the book of Ruth. God blessed Naomi's daughter-in-law, Ruth, who brought hope and restoration to Naomi. Long story short, Ruth worked in a field to support herself and Naomi. She met a man named Boaz. Through a series of events, Boaz restored to Ruth and Naomi all they had lost, taking them into his protection, into his family, and into his heart.

This love story is a picture of God's heart of love for us.

When we're stuck in the loss, in the hard, in the grief, we struggle to hold onto hope. It can take a long time to get to a happy ending, to have any sort of peace or perspective about the trials and tragedies we've experienced. We struggle to see how our trials can be part of God's plan for our lives. Like Naomi, it's so easy to drift into bitter waters of anger, depression, or hopelessness.

But God can bring "Ruths" and "Boazes" into your life to encourage you in these difficult days, months, years. This is the vital importance of real relationships. If we are open, no matter how reluctantly, God can use others in our lives to restore hope and bring us back to him.

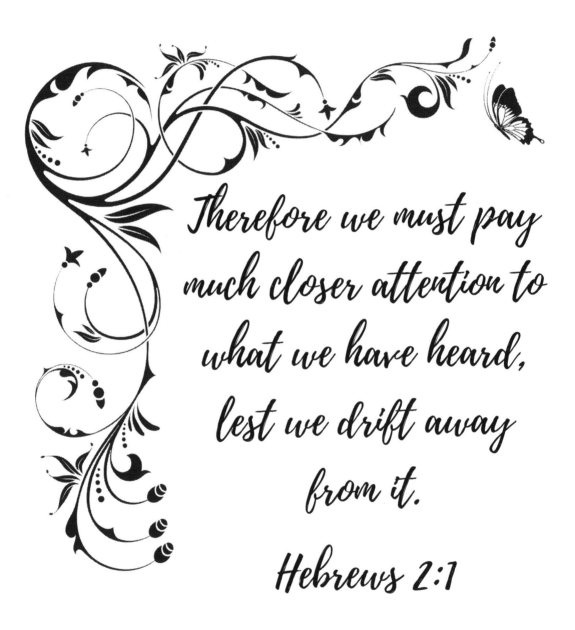

Therefore we must pay much closer attention to what we have heard, lest we drift away from it.

Hebrews 2:1

WEEK THREE

Holding Fast in the Storms of Life

I'm not the type of person who enjoys pain. I'd much rather relax on the couch, binge watch my favorite show, and eat chocolate instead of train for a marathon. Intellectually, I know if I want to become leaner, faster, and stronger, I'm going to have to hold fast to my workout schedule, fight for healthy nutrition, and persevere in the face of temptation. Emotionally, I don't feel like doing it.

Too often, I fight the hard and give in to what's comfortable.

Toughing It Up

The military is different. Hard is often right. "There's no crying in uniform." Suck it up, and get it done. Yet it goes beyond this hard exterior. Lofty ideals and grander purposes motivate us to run towards the fight and embrace the suck.

Below are some of the Armed Forces' mottos:
- *Semper Fidelis (Always Faithful)*
- *Aim High…Fly-Fight-Win*
- *This We'll Defend*

- *Semper Fortis (Always Strong)*
- *Semper Paratus (Always Ready)*

These ideals call us to persevere in battle. There is something worth fighting for. In the Christian life, we will face hardships. Jesus promises us that we will experience trouble (John 16:33). Similar to military combat, perseverance will be the difference between victory and defeat, progress and stagnation. There is something worth fighting for.

Bible Truth

The Bible often speaks to this idea.

> *Not only that, but we rejoice in our sufferings, knowing that suffering produces endurance, and endurance produces character, and character produces hope, and hope does not put us to shame, because God's love has been poured out into our hearts through the Holy Spirit who has been given to us. —Romans 5:3-5*

> *"Count it all joy, my brothers, when you meet trials of various kinds, for you know that the testing of your faith produces steadfastness. And let steadfastness have its full effect, that you may be perfect and complete, lacking in nothing. — James 1:2-4*

> *"Beloved, do not be surprised at the fiery trial when it comes upon you to test you, as though something strange were happening to you. But rejoice insofar as you share Christ's sufferings, that you may also rejoice and be glad when his glory is revealed. —1 Peter 4:12-13*

While mottos are inspiring and motivating, they are sometimes inadequate. Jesus gives us something better. He gives us hope. He promises that our difficulty in this world is not without purpose.

Adversity helps us grow.

The writer of Hebrews understood this and sought to encourage his readers to hold fast while suffering. To trust and hope, not in their circumstances, but in God's character. He understood that pure grit and determination are insufficient weapons in the war of life.

We can only carry ourselves so far. Battle buddies can help to an extent. But to overcome and remain faithful to the end, we need someone better. We need Jesus. He is the only one who can give us the strength we need to endure. He is the only one who can provide complete comfort when life beats us down. He is the only one who can give us a higher purpose in our pain. He is the only one who can create beauty out of shrapnel.[11]

If we're going to persevere in this world and grow up to be more like Christ, we need to focus on Jesus, looking to him for our strength, anchoring ourselves in his character.

---

[11] Isaiah 61:3

43

HOMEWORK

In your homework this week, we will discuss how trust, soul care, and the importance of a Sabbath rest help us hold fast.

DAY 1: HOLDING FAST

An anchor is a vital piece of gear on a ship. There are many types of anchors, each with a variety of purposes. Some limit speed, controlling drift in a storm. Others secure a vessel to a mooring permanently.

To maximize efficiency, anchors work in tandem with many things. They either hook into the seabed, hold the ship by its sheer mass, or some combination of the two.[12]

I know you're wondering where I'm going with this. I assure you I have not suddenly found a passion for maritime trivia. I believe there are parallels to our walk with God.

While the imagery of an anchor occurs only once in the Bible (Hebrews 6:19), the idea of being anchored to God is a concept found throughout Scripture. One of the terms for this is "hold fast." In the Greek, the phrase "hold fast" means to hold down, to have, to keep in memory, to possess, seize on, stay.[13] This phrase appears eight times in Scripture; four of those in Hebrews. Let's take a peek at the first mention of it in the book of Hebrews.

1. In the verses below, underline the words "hold fast." Circle what we are to hold fast and what we are to boast in.

> *Now Moses was faithful in all God's house as a servant, to testify to the things that were to be spoken later, but Christ is faithful over God's house as a son. And we are his house, if indeed we hold fast our confidence and our boasting in our hope. —Hebrews 3:5-6*

---

[12] https://en.wikipedia.org/wiki/Anchor
[13] https://www.blueletterbible.org/lang/lexicon/lexicon.cfm?Strongs=G2722&t=KJV

44

How is Christ's faithfulness as God's son better than Moses's faithfulness as God's servant?

We've already talked about our propensity to drift. Fast currents, stormy waters, and faulty navigation can all lead to disaster. To remain afloat and prevent drift (or worse, capsizing), we need to drop anchor in a secure seabed. For a believer, we must "hold fast" to the character of God.

That is our confidence and our hope.

In Week One, we spent a good deal of time looking at the attributes of Jesus as defined by the book of Hebrews. Today, we look at the whole of God's character to better understand why we should anchor ourselves in him. If this feels repetitive, it is intentional. We are a forgetful people, especially in times of suffering. We must fix our gaze on God and who he is.

So who does God say he is?

In the Old Testament, one of the first mentions of how God identifies himself occurs in Exodus. Before leading the children of Israel into the Promised Land, Moses asked God to reveal himself. God responds by passing in front of Moses and proclaiming his name.

2. Write out Exodus 34:6-7. Underline God's character traits.

I dread election years. Listening to empty promises from politicians is not my idea of fun. Could you connect any empty promises to the traits you underlined? Thankfully, God is nothing like a politician.

3. Look up Hebrews 10:23. What are we to hold fast? Why can we trust God?

The value of the promise rests in the character of the promisor.

God is faithful. He is trustworthy. We can take him at his word because he never changes, always tells the truth, is in control, and loves us with an unwavering, steadfast kind of love.

It's easy to believe that when life is good. What about when challenges arise? When we suffer, it's tempting to interpret what's happening to us as a lack of love on God's part.

I miscarried in the middle of a PCS before I knew anyone at my new duty station. I questioned God. I was angry with him, not just for letting my baby die, but for allowing him/her to die before I even had a support system to carry me through it. I felt incredibly isolated and alone. I grieved for months.

Friends from other places sent me cards, books, encouraging words, flowers. Nothing helped. I was beginning to lose hope. Ironically enough, the only place I found comfort was in a deep-dive study of God's character. It wasn't exactly intentional. I went searching for friends and ended up in a Bible study that was all about who God is. The intense study of his character answered my questions and gave me peace.

That horrible event in my life deepened my relationship with God. Though it feels trite to write, I'm thankful for the pain of my miscarriage because it brought me so much closer to the Lord. I matured in my faith, just as God promised.

4. Have you had a similar experience when you felt something terrible was happening to you and that God didn't love you? How did you respond? How do you think studying God's character might help you re-frame your negative experiences?

5. Psalm 86 is a prayer David prayed while suffering. Read it and notice how he reminds himself of God's character. Use some of David's words to write your own prayer, asking God to help you in your current circumstances, reminding yourself of who God is.

DAY 2: TRUST

The book of Hebrews contains several warnings. The harder life gets, the more prone we are to wander.

God's people – the Israelites – were a picture of this. After God delivered them from slavery in Egypt, he led them through the desert to the Promised Land. Although they could have taken a shortcut, God instructed them to follow a different path (Exodus 13:17), and they began to complain. God provided for their every need, but they could not see it. They focused on what they didn't have and what life used to be like.

When it came time for them to enter the Promised Land, they were too afraid. They did not trust that God could give them this land where a horde of fierce, intimidating people already lived. Rather than holding fast to God, they rebelled against him. Eventually, God had enough of it. He decided none of the people who came out of Egypt would go into the Promised Land. They would instead wander in the desert for forty years (see Numbers 32:1-13).

In Hebrews 3, we find a retelling of this story, a warning to not do what the Israelites did.

1. Look up Hebrews 3:12-14.

What is the warning? (v. 12)	
How do we combat this? (v. 13)	
What guarantees that we are sharing in Christ? (v. 14)	

That word, "hold" in Hebrews 3:14 is the same word used in the verses we looked up yesterday. It's a reminder to persevere, to remember the truth of who God is and what he has done.

Let's keep reading in Hebrews 3 to find out what happens when we don't hold fast to God and his character.

2. Read Hebrews 3:15-19. Write out verse 19. What prevented the people of Israel from being able to enter the Promised Land?

Yesterday, we looked at God's character. If all those things are true about God, why do we still struggle to trust him? Could it be that we, like the Israelites, focus on our circumstances instead of on God's character?

I know that was true for me when I miscarried. As long as I focused on what happened, I struggled to trust God.

Over and over again, the Bible tells us that we must have faith. Hebrews 11:1 defines faith for us.

3. Read Hebrews 11:1. Paraphrase it in your own words.

Faith requires us to know God, not just know about him. The better and more accurate our view of Christ, the easier it will be to trust him. The amount of our faith matters little. The object of our faith matters much.

4. What situation is currently making it difficult for you to trust God?

5. Write out a prayer asking God to help you with your unbelief and trust him more deeply in your circumstances.

DAY 3: SOUL CARE

Let us therefore strive to enter that rest, so that no one may fall by the same sort of disobedience.
—*Hebrews 4:10*

Self-care is a prevalent idea in our culture. As military women, we are often overwhelmed, stressed, and exhausted. The notion of a "day off" sounds amazing but unattainable.

How do you rest in the middle of a deployment?
How do you stop working when you have kids, mountains of laundry, dirty floors, and meals to cook?

The idea of "Sabbath" – to cease working for a day – is not meant to give us one more task to check off in the Christian life. It is a gift to restore us and give us the strength to keep going. But it goes beyond self-care.

While going for a run or exploring local venues may help you break out of the routine and give you a boost, the boost doesn't last. As soon as you get home or back on duty, all the work is still right there waiting for you. That doesn't mean we shouldn't do those things. It's just a reality.

Perhaps it just means our souls need care too.

So for me, when I do one of those "self-care" things, I try to pair it with something spiritual as well:

- *listening to worship music or a podcast on my way to do something I enjoy*
- *memorizing verses while I sip a delicious drink*
- *working out with friends who tell me about how God is working in their lives*

I find that when I do these things, I'm a little less empty when I return home.

Not all seasons of military life allow us to take days off. We must be women who are intentional about finding those pockets of time to rest rather than waste.

1. What does a "no-work" day look like for you? How can you tie it to something spiritual?

Another way we can care for our souls is by remembering what God has done for us. When our focus shifts towards heaven, we cease striving here on earth. We can finally rest.

Remembering helps us hold fast.

> *For I brought you up from the land of Egypt and redeemed you from the house of slavery, and I sent before you Moses, Aaron, and Miriam. O my people, **remember** what Balak king of Moab devised, and what Balaam the son of Beor answered him, and what happened from Shittim to Gilgal, **that you may know the righteous acts of the** LORD. —Micah 6:4-5, emphasis added*

Remembering what God has done in our lives and in the lives of those around us strengthens our faith. God knows this, which is why he instituted special provisions so that his people would remember.

2. Fill in the chart below. The first one is an example

Verse	Method of Remembering	What were they to remember?
Exodus 12:43-51	Passover	That God delivered them from slavery
Deuteronomy 5:15		
Joshua 4:1-7		
Luke 22:19-20		

Though we are no longer commanded to keep the feasts as the Jewish people did in the Old Testament, we can draw on the principle behind it. Setting up times and methods of remembering God's faithfulness is essential if we are to hold fast to God's character and find his rest.

When we struggle, we need to remember God's faithfulness. Recalling how he worked during a previous trial will give us the strength we need to endure and rest in the midst of heartache.

3. What are some ways you can cause yourself to remember what God has done for you? What are some ways you can share that with others?

4. What are some other ways to rest in God?

DAY 4: A SABBATH REST

On Day Two, we talked about the Israelites' journey to the Promised Land.

Let's focus on that aspect of Promised Land today – on what awaits us when we hold fast to God. The Old Testament often describes the Promised Land as "a land flowing with milk and honey" (Numbers 14:8, Deuteronomy 31:20, Joshua 5:6).

For the Hebrews, it was to be a land of rest. A place where they were no longer slaves, no longer nomads, but could instead enjoy abundance, peace, and stability. True to the theme, the author of Hebrews tells us that there is a better rest than what the Israelites experienced because someone better than Moses gives it to us.

1. Read Hebrews 4:8-10. What type of rest remains for the people of God (v. 9)?

The word Sabbath in this passage refers to "the blessed rest from toils and troubles looked for in the age to come by the true worshippers of God and true Christians."[14]

While we are not promised an easy life here on earth, we have the promise of an eternity of rest - a place without death, a place without pain, a place without tears (Revelation 21:5). If we hold fast to this idea - that this is our future - it will make our present experience endurable. The problem again is when we, like the Israelites, do not believe.

This Sabbath rest is not just a futuristic goal. It can be a present reality—if we hold fast. We can be at rest, at peace, regardless of what our circumstances look like.

2. Is your Christian experience a wilderness experience or a Promised Land experience?

---

[14] https://www.blueletterbible.org/lang/lexicon/lexicon.cfm?Strongs=G4520&t=KJV

When we trust in our resources, our abilities, our success, we will struggle.

As military women, we want to fight. We are an action-oriented group. We don't surrender. Ironically, Jesus calls us to an upside-down life. A countercultural life. He tells us to be still and know that he is God (Psalm 46:10).

The Bible says things like, "The battle is the Lord's" (1 Samuel 17:47, 2 Chronicles 20:15). God doesn't ask us to fight. He just asks us to believe. When we become women who surrender and trust that God is in control, then we can truly rest and enjoy what he has for us. Even through pain and heartache.

3. In what ways are you currently trying to make a difficult situation better? How can you surrender and trust that God will fight that battle for you?

DAY 5: ACCOUNTABLE TOGETHER

I recently went to a newcomer's luncheon at my installation. One of the speakers asked each of us to write down 1-2 challenges we face in military life. The most common answer was "establishing relationships in a new place."

Whether we're introverts or extroverts, we need other people to help us hold fast to God—especially when life is tough.

The warnings laced throughout Hebrews often incorporate this concept of community. Let's go back to a passage we looked at yesterday, but read it with a different lens.

1. Read Hebrews 3:12-13. How can other people help us hold fast to God?

2. What does it mean to exhort one another?

Reread Hebrews 3:13.

Notice that we are to be careful of the deceitfulness of sin. We do not often see ourselves accurately. Sin is cunning. We need others to speak truth into our lives, to hold us accountable.

> The Hebrews passage clearly teaches that personal insight is the product of community. I need you in order to really see and know myself. Otherwise, I will listen to my own arguments, believe my own lies, and buy into my own delusions. My self-perception is as accurate as a carnival mirror. If I am going to see myself clearly, I need you to hold the mirror of God's Word in front of me. —Paul David Tripp[15]

3. Who in your life can hold up the mirror of God's Word to you? How can you hold up the mirror of God's Word to others?

We need other people to hold us accountable and encourage us not to give up, to keep going. The Bible compares our lives to a race. Just as runners need encouragers to hold up signs, shout affirmations, and offer a high-five, we need other believers to do that for us spiritually.

4. Read Hebrews 12:1. What is the cloud of witnesses? (See Hebrews 11) How can reading and hearing about the lives of other believers encourage us to persevere in our own lives?

---

[15] Paul David Tripp, *Instruments in the Redeemer's Hands: People in Need of Change Helping People in Need of Change* (Phillipsburg, New Jersey: P&R Publishing, 2002), p. 54.

H20: GRATITUDE*

There was an article circulating my social media feed a few weeks back on the brain research behind gratitude. The headline read, "Neuroscience Reveals: Gratitude Literally Rewires Your Brain to be Happier."[16]

While it might be the trendy thing to do these days, the Bible has been talking about it for thousands of years.

> *Oh give thanks to the LORD, for he is good; for his steadfast love endures forever.* —1 Chronicles 16:34

> *Offer to God a sacrifice of thanksgiving, and perform your vows to the Most High.* —Psalm 50:14

> *Give thanks in all circumstances; for this is the will of God in Christ Jesus for you.* —1 Thessalonians 5:18

Biblical gratitude turns one's attention from the gift to the Giver. So as you begin the habit of gratitude, think about how you can tie it back to God.

- Start a gratitude journal.
- List at least three things each day for which you are thankful. Research shows the best times to do this are either morning or night.
- Begin incorporating the items in a prayer of thanksgiving.

*H20 stands for Habits to Outcome. Each week we will introduce a particular spiritual discipline to help you grow and better apply the concepts of this Bible study.

---

[16] https://dailyhealthpost.com/gratitude-rewires-brain-happier/?utm_source=link&utm_medium=fb&utm_campaign=sq&utm_content=dhp, accessed 11/29/19.

DIGGING DEEPER: CONNECTING WITH HEROES OF THE FAITH

Holding fast to who God is in the midst of tragedy and turmoil is no easy feat. While no one does it correctly 100% of the time, there is someone in the Bible from whom we can take a few cues.

Growing up, he was the favorite son. His father didn't try to hide it, gifting his son with a coat meant for a king. His brothers became insanely jealous. Many of us joke about selling our siblings, but they did just that.

Joseph was probably just a teenager when it happened. His father sent him to check on his brothers, who were out in the field watching the flocks. They weren't too keen on seeing him. After all, this was the kid who told them they were going to bow down to him one day. Their first instinct was to kill him, but one of the more rational brothers (Reuben) convinced the others to instead throw him in a pit. Reuben planned to come back and rescue Joseph, but he somehow missed hearing about their plan to sell Joseph to a traveling caravan. When he went back to the pit, Joseph was gone. The brothers went home and told their father a wild animal attacked Joseph, showing his torn, bloody coat as evidence.

Joseph was sold into slavery and began to work in the household of one of the most powerful men in Egypt – Potiphar. Potiphar's wife tried to seduce Joseph, then accused him of trying to take advantage of her. Potiphar put Joseph in prison, where he served a ten-year sentence. Though he distinguished himself as a leader and received the promise of release, he was forgotten. Two years later, he got the opportunity to interpret a dream for Pharaoh. This finally won him his freedom and a promotion to second-in-command in Egypt. Throughout all these trials, Joseph held fast to his faith in God. He forgave his brothers and pointed back to God.

"As for you, you meant evil against me, but God meant it for good, to bring it about that many people should be kept alive, as they are today. So do not fear; I will provide for you and your little ones." Thus he comforted them and spoke kindly to them. —Genesis 50:20-21

The Bible doesn't give us complete insight into how Joseph felt during all these trials. I'm sure there were times he struggled, just like we do. How did he remain hopeful? How did he persevere? Based on what he says at the end of his story, I believe it's because he trusted God and his character. He understood that God was able to bring good out of evil. He held fast to who God is. Even when our circumstances look hopeless, we can hold fast to God and who he is - trusting that he is working good for us even in our pain.

We have this as a sure and steadfast anchor of the soul, a hope that enters into the inner places behind the curtain.

Hebrews 6:19

WEEK FOUR

Encouragement

And let us consider how to stir up one another to love and good works, not neglecting to meet together as is the habit of some, but encouraging one another, and all the more as you see the Day drawing near. —Hebrews 10:24-25

Military life can be discouraging in so many different ways. Consider the following challenges:

- canceled leave
- assignment changes
- extended deployments
- casualty notifications
- housing issues
- childcare struggles
- toxic leadership

It is easy to become disappointed and disheartened. PSTD and depression infiltrate our ranks. Suicide is now the second leading cause of death in the U.S. military.[17]

---

[17] https://deploymentpsych.org/disorders/suicide-main, accessed 11/25/19

We are women deeply in need of encouragement, surrounded by other women deeply needing support.

Finding Hope in a Hopeless World

The writer of Hebrews knew a little something about the need for hope in a hopeless world. He wrote to a group of Jewish people undergoing harsh oppression and persecution. All along, his message was "hold fast."

But now he builds on that idea, shedding light on another way to persevere – through community. He even writes it in a way that encourages brotherhood and sisterhood.

Rather than instructing *them* to do something, he includes himself – "let us consider how to stir up one another…encouraging one another…" The message here is two-fold. We need to encourage others, but we also need to be in a community where we can be supported.

Persevere in Community

In the military, we shift our identity. Rather than distinguishing ourselves as individuals, we classify ourselves as members of a greater whole, all working towards a common goal.

Christianity is similar. When we become Christians, God adopts us into his family. We become brothers and sisters with others who believe in Jesus. The Bible calls this "the body of Christ" (Romans 12:5, 1 Corinthians 12:12-27).

Our identity moves from individuals to members of a family or body. As members of the body, we are all running a race – growing to be like Jesus. Without the encouragement of fellow believers, we will struggle to reach the finish line. Just as you would not let your running mate fall out, so we, as Christians, should not allow our brothers and sisters in Christ to become discouraged. Never leave a fellow soldier (sailor, airman, Marine, coastguardsman) behind.

We are uniquely qualified to do this. No one understands a military woman quite like another military woman. But if we are too immature in our walk or too inward-focused, we may miss a chance to spur another woman on in her journey with Jesus. And we could miss an opportunity to find ourselves encouraged.

HOMEWORK

In your homework this week, we will reflect on the importance of encouragement in our lives and the lives of those in our community.

And let us consider how to stir up one another to love and good works, not neglecting to meet together as is the habit of some, but encouraging one another, and all the more as you see the Day drawing near. —Hebrews 10:24-25

DAY 1: THE CORE OF OUR ENCOURAGEMENT

Before we can encourage others, we must first understand the source of sincere, biblical hope and encouragement. Once again, we turn to the book of Hebrews.

1. Read Hebrews 10:19-25. Complete the blanks below.

Since we have a_____ (v. 19)

Since we have a _____ (v. 21)

Let us _____ (v. 22)

Let us _____ (v. 23)

And let us _____ (v.24)

2. According to these verses, why can we have confidence, full assurance of faith, and hope?

3. How does believing verses 19-21 enable us to act out verses 22-24?

When you are going through something difficult, what do you want people to say to you? Do you want reassurance that it will be ok? That it will all work out in the end?

How many times have you heard that everything will be okay, only to realize later that things were not ok? We need something beyond human words of encouragement. We need something better – the hope and encouragement that come from Jesus Christ, the Son of God.

Hebrews 7:23 tell us that because of Jesus, we now have complete access to God. We have an advocate, someone who always intercedes on our behalf (Romans 8:34).

We no longer need to fear God's wrath or judgment. He set his love upon us, and nothing can separate us from it. That is what gives us confidence, full assurance, and hope.

4. How does knowing that you have unlimited access to God, full access to all that he is – his love, his faithfulness, his grace, his mercy - give you hope and encouragement?

DAY 2: IDENTIFY THE STRUGGLE

I am a planner and a list-maker. But when I'm stressed and overwhelmed, I go into survival mode. I do the bare minimum for what is required to get me through the day.

When hard times come, and I struggle to persevere, planning and list-making disappear from my life. Intentionality morphs into survivability.

During a trial, I also become incredibly inward-focused. I think only of myself and my microscopic world. Seldom do I consider others and what they may be going through or what they need. The author of Hebrews seems to understand this tendency, which is why he writes Hebrews 10:24.

1. Look up Hebrews 10:24. Write the first four words.

The Greek word for "consider" means to "consider attentively, to fix one's eyes or mind upon."[18] We are not to be women who think only of ourselves, who approach life with a "what's the point?" attitude. Instead, we are to focus our mental energy on how we can build up others. We are to be intentional – deliberately and purposefully encouraging those around us.

To consider how to stir up or encourage others, we need to contemplate what is going on in their world.

Where are they struggling?
What is their need?

---

[18] https://www.blueletterbible.org/lang/lexicon/lexicon.cfm?Strongs=G2657&t=KJV, accessed 11/27/19

Vague encouragement and platitudes do not minister to a woman dealing with her husband's affair or with the death of a child. If we are to offer genuine, biblical encouragement, we need first to consider their situation. Then we can see how to show them the hope that Jesus promises, applying it directly to their specific circumstances.

Empathy and connection require us to humble ourselves — to put others' needs before our own.

2. Read Philippians 2:3-4. Who is someone you can consider more significant than yourself today? How can you encourage that person in their struggle?

Have you noticed that when you encourage someone else, it lifts your mood as well? While it may seem backward to us to take care of others' needs before our own, God knows this is the better way.

3. After you encourage that person you wrote about in question 2, come back and journal what happened and how it inspired you.

DAY 3: STRENGTH IN DIVERSITY

There are numerous ways to encourage others. Don't get the impression from yesterday's homework that there is only one way to inspire others.

1. Look up 1 Thessalonians 5:11. What synonym for *encourages* is used?

> THAT THEIR HEARTS MAY BE ENCOURAGED, BEING KNIT TOGETHER IN LOVE, TO REACH ALL THE RICHES OF FULL ASSURANCE OF UNDERSTANDING AND THE KNOWLEDGE OF GOD'S MYSTERY, WHICH IS CHRIST (COLOSSIANS 2:2).

Are you familiar with the concept of love languages?[19] If not, I highly suggest you take a few minutes to visit the Five Love Languages website to learn about them or read *Five Love Languages Military Edition: The Secret to Love that Lasts.* These languages though originally applied to romantic relationships, have since been expanded to include parent-child relationships, spiritual and work relationships, and friendships.

In seeking to encourage others, consider learning the love language of the person you want to build up. For example, if someone speaks quality time, you could call or hang out with them, finding out what's going on in their lives. If someone enjoys small tokens or gifts, you could bring a little "thinking about you" present over to their house or send it in the mail. For someone who enjoys words of affirmation, you can say, "I saw you do _____, and it was really _____." Specificity makes all the difference.

---

[19] https://www.5lovelanguages.com/

2. Think about the love languages of those around you. Using their unique language, write down two ideas for how to build them up this week. Then make it a point to implement at least one of those ideas.

When we're in the trenches, discouraged, and downtrodden, a shift in perspective can be helpful. That's something we can do for one another – remind each other of what we're living for, what's to come in the future, the place we have in God's kingdom.

3. Read Hebrews 12:1-3 below. Underline the words describing what Jesus focused on during his time on earth.

Therefore, since we are surrounded by so great a cloud of witnesses, let us also lay aside every weight, and sin which clings so closely, and let us run with endurance the race that is set before us, looking to Jesus, the founder and perfecter of our faith, who for the joy set before him endured the cross, despising the shame, and is seated at the right hand of God.

Jesus kept his eyes on heaven, on the higher purpose behind what he was doing. We, too, need to remember that we are part of a grander story. God's purpose for us in this world is much higher than what the world tells us.

We need to be women who can lift our eyes – beyond the mess, the mission, and the mundane.

But to do this, we need other people.

4. Look back at Hebrews 12:1-3. Circle the words that describe who surrounds us. In context, this refers back to Hebrews 11, where several Old Testament characters' lives highlight their faith in God.

Right now, we are all part of someone else's "cloud of witnesses." What are we doing to remind them of the joy that is set before them?

5. What are some ways you can encourage someone in your life with the bigger picture of what's to come?

DAY 4: THE PURPOSE OF ENCOURAGEMENT

Encouragement is the fuel we all need when life gets hard. As stated earlier, biblical encouragement differs from the world's definition of encouragement.

1. Look up the word encouragement and write the meaning below.

When we talk about biblical encouragement, the definition changes slightly. "Believers can encourage one another to have greater confidence in God and so to be bold in living out their faith."[20]

In essence, this is what the book of Hebrews is – a letter to encourage Christians to

- Know that Jesus is more significant (and thus, have greater confidence in him).
- Choose bold faith, persevering through suffering and persecution. "I appeal to you, brothers, bear with my word of **exhortation**, for I have written to you briefly" (Hebrews 13:22, emphasis added).

---

[20] https://biblehub.com/topical/dbt/8415.htm, accessed 11/28/19

Both the Old and New Testaments are full of examples that flesh out this idea of encouraging others.

2. Fill in the table below. The first one is done for you as an example.

Verses	Encourager	Encouraged	Method of Encouragement	Result
2 Chronicles 32:6-8	King Hezekiah	Combat commanders and soldiers	Spoken – pointing to God's help	They took confidence in God and were bold to fight despite fear
1 Samuel 23:16-18				
Acts 11:22-24				
1 Thessalonians 3:6-7				

Encouragement takes on many forms. Whether it's pouring courage into frightened, insecure soldiers, comforting persecuted missionaries with stories of new faith, or just being present with a friend during a challenging season, encouragement is a vital part of a believer's life.

3. Think through the examples from the table above. What are some ways you can encourage those around you to have greater confidence in God and boldly live out their faith?

DAY 5: ENCOURAGING TOGETHER

One of the most significant advantages of military life is the ability to see different parts of the world and meet a variety of people.

Instead of growing up in the same church my entire life, I had the privilege of experiencing an assortment of churches, denominations, Bible study groups, and ministries. Each one added to my faith in a unique way.

In a church in Arizona, I learned how to study the Bible verse-by-verse. In a community group in Georgia, I discovered what it looked like to meet another's needs out of love. Yet another body of believers in Germany taught me how to communicate and explain biblical themes.

Had I chosen not to take part in these faith communities, I would not have grown in my walk with God. I would have remained immature and ineffective in my Christian witness.

1. Read Hebrews 10:24-25. What are we **not** to do? What are we to do instead?

These verses in Hebrews address our need to meet regularly with other believers for two purposes.

2. Write the two goals in your own words.

While choosing to interact with other believers is not always easy or convenient, it is vital to our spiritual growth.

We need each other.

The Bible teaches that mutual encouragement is a by-product of the Christian community. "For I long to see you, that I may impart to you some spiritual gift to strengthen you – that is, that we may be **mutually encouraged** by each other's faith, both yours and mine" (Romans 1:11-12, emphasis added).

I have always been a quiet, reserved person, choosing to remain in the background and observe. Through my years of observation, I have learned much from other people, particularly other Christians. Seeing how they sacrificially give to worthy causes or gently correct their children encourages me to grow in these areas.

3. How have you been encouraged by someone else's faith?

4. What are some ways you can stir up another believer's faith?

A man named Paul wrote much of the New Testament. (You might remember his story from Week 1, Heroes of the Faith.) He was a man steeped in the community. Relationships mattered deeply to him. He especially poured his heart and soul into a younger believer named Timothy – teaching, training, and guiding him.

Mentoring relationships can be an influential source of mutual encouragement.

5. Think through the people in your life. Who can be your Paul? Who can be your Timothy?

6. Write down at least two things you can do this week to encourage your Timothy.

H20: VERSE MEMORIZATION*

Have you ever been grocery shopping and realized you forgot your list at home? You try to remember what you wrote. A few things come to mind, and you wander the aisles hoping to jog your memory. You get as many groceries as you remember you needed, plus a few impulse-buys, and head home. When you get back to your list, you realize you forgot the main ingredients for tonight's meal!

Sometimes we can be in conversation with people and remember parts of a verse we read in the Bible that would be so appropriate to what we're talking about, but we can't remember enough to actually share about it. Wouldn't it be great if we could hold verses in our hearts and minds so that we could encourage those around us? "Preach the word; be ready in season and out of season; reprove, rebuke, and exhort, with complete patience and teaching" (2 Timothy 4:2).

Here are a few tips to help you memorize Bible verses:

- Write down the verse(s) you want to memorize and display it prominently. Take it with you throughout your day.
- Rehearse phrase by phrase, out loud if possible.
- Say the reference (where the verse is found) at the beginning and end.
- Turn it into a prayer back to God.
- Review frequently.

*H20 stands for Habits to Outcome. Each week we will introduce a particular spiritual discipline to help you grow and better apply the concepts of this Bible study.

DIGGING DEEPER: CONNECTING WITH HEROES OF THE FAITH

Isn't it refreshing to find out the meaning behind people's names? In the Bible, names are incredibly significant. Our English translations often forfeit their connotations, but every once in a while, we gain some insight.

In Acts 4:36, we meet a man named Joseph, but the apostles call him Barnabas, which means "son of encouragement." Though stories about him are sprinkled throughout the book of Acts, much can be learned from his example – and his name! Barnabas was one of the first men to accept Paul after his conversion. Everyone else was terrified of the known assassin, but Barnabas brought him to the apostles and told them how Jesus changed Paul's life.

From that point on, the apostles accepted him as one of their own. Barnabas, like Paul, was a missionary and steady pillar of the New Testament church. The Bible describes him as "a good man, full of the Holy Spirit and of faith" (Acts 11:24).

He was a man well versed in encouraging others. Throughout the book of Acts, we find many examples of this. First, he urged the church at Antioch to persevere and hold fast (Acts 11:23). He also traveled with Paul to other churches, speaking out the truth of the gospel (Acts 12:25, 15:2), and he heartened congregations with news about the signs and wonders God performed (Acts 15:12).

In everything he did, Barnabas worked for the good of those around them. Through his words of encouragement, he built others up, gave them greater confidence in God, and made them bold in their faith.

It wasn't always easy for Barnabas. Like Paul, he fought against the Jews' wrong teaching (Acts 15:2). He struggled in relationships, eventually separating from Paul to minister in Cyprus (Acts 15:39). He was no stranger to persecution and suffering (Acts 13:50). In spite of all of this, he remained faithful to the Lord and his brothers and sisters in Christ.

As we've seen this week, encouragement is an essential part of our journey as believers. Living in a community with others reveals this beautiful gift. So, let's be women who choose to engage each other with intentionality and humility.

Now may our Lord Jesus Christ himself, and God our Father, who loved us and gave us eternal comfort and good hope through grace, comfort your hearts and establish them in every good work and word.

2 Thessalonians 2:16-17

WEEK FIVE

Love and Good Works

Let us Consider How to Love

I recently returned from a visit with my family. In military life, those visits can be hard to come by, which makes them even more special and memorable.

There's nothing better than spending time with those you love and those who love you. Those moments fill us with warm, cozy feelings that inspire, motivate, and challenge us. I wish I could have friendships that do the same thing. But moving around every few years makes it difficult. Just when you find friends it's time to leave.

Can I be honest? Sometimes I wish there were parts of the Bible with a parenthetical statement that reads, "does not apply to the military." Like these verses in Hebrews 10: "And let us consider how to stir up one another to love and good works, not neglecting to meet together, as is the habit of some, but encouraging one another, and all the more as you see the Day drawing near"(24-25).

Unfortunately, the "does not apply to the military" clause is missing; we are not exempt. Though it is painful when we relocate, God knows the value relationships have on our lives and our spiritual growth. Other people draw something out of us that we don't naturally exhibit when we're by ourselves. Likewise, we bring out in other people qualities they would not instinctively demonstrate on their own.

The Hebrew writer understood that as individuals, we become lazy, selfish, and unloving.

We need each other to grow – to stir us up!

Some translations use the words stimulate, spur on, or provoke. The writer of Hebrews understood that there is a type of positive peer pressure that exists in Christian communities. When we intentionally engage with other believers, we will learn from one another.

Love the Unlovable

> WHOEVER WALKS WITH THE WISE BECOMES WISE, BUT THE COMPANION OF FOOLS WILL SUFFER HARM (PROVERBS 13:20).

Two of the things we learn from each other, according to this verse, are love and good works. It's easy to imagine how you can pick up these positive traits in a community of people where you feel connected, supported, and encouraged. But what about being in a group with unlovable, difficult people – the ones who grate on your nerves? Can we become versed in love and good works with people like that?

God intentionally places people in our lives to mold us into his image – to look like Jesus.

Be More like Jesus

While we would rather avoid some of them, God is faithful to use all circumstances and people for our good. Perhaps the more burdensome people in our lives are the very ones who will provoke us to love and good works in more profound, more significant ways.

After all, the goal is to grow to be more like Jesus. When we look at his life, we see his friends and companions were not the most likable people. Yet still, he loved them. The amazing thing about Jesus is that he didn't just come to earth to die for us. If he had, that certainly would have been enough—a sincere act of the most sacrificial kind of love you can find. He also came to earth to live among us—to be God with us. Us—the people who rebel against his commands, flaunting them in his face. Let's accept it. We're not lovable people. But somehow, the God of the universe treasures us and wants to be with us. How amazing is that?!

In his great love for us, God desires that we will care for others in that same way. "By this all people will know that you are my disciples, if you have love for one another" (John 13:35).

HOMEWORK

In your homework this week, we will draw from the example of Jesus to love others as he loved us.

And let us consider how to stir up one another to love and good works, not neglecting to meet together as is the habit of some, but encouraging one another, and all the more as you see the Day drawing near. —Hebrews 10:24-25

DAY 1: LOVE LIKE JESUS

Have you ever been told to do something only to have no idea how to do it? It's incredibly frustrating and overwhelming. I'm the type of person who wants to know how to perform a task, with a rubric, past examples, and a due date.

The military produces Standard Operating Procedures (SOPs). While not always up to date, it's at least an attempt to standardize the process by which we do things. Those written rules and step-by-step instructions help us perform routine, yet complicated tasks.[21]

When it comes to love, we want an SOP; but what we get is something even better. We get a person. Throughout the book of Hebrews, the writer has been reminding us that Jesus is better. Jesus modeled how to love all people – those we like and those we don't like. He left us instructions, but he also practiced what he preached.

1. Look up the following passages and describe how Jesus showed love to others.

---

[21] https://en.wikipedia.org/wiki/Standard_operating_procedure, accessed 12/3/19.

Passage	Description
John 13:1-15	
Matthew 14:14	
Mark 6:34	

2. How do Matthew and Mark define love? To what kind of love does John refer?

Compassion and service were two significant aspects of the love Jesus showed others. I often think, "Sure, it was easy for Jesus to love. He's God. God is love." But Jesus was fully man as well as fully God. He still had to choose to love. He had to persevere when love was hard. Consider the people in the passages you just read.

3. In John 13:1-15, who is the unlovable person? Hint: it's not Peter.

Can you imagine serving someone who is about to betray you? That is the kind of love that Jesus shows.

The other two passages describe crowds. Remember that I'm an introvert, so the thought of having compassion for a group of people is beyond me. Crowds are noisy, rude, disorganized, and unruly. Yet Jesus cared for them deeply. I have a lot of growing to do.

4. Think about how you love others. In what ways do you need to grow to be more like Jesus in this area?

It's sobering to realize how much growth still needs to occur in our journey as believers, especially in the area of loving others. But remember, Jesus is better! He gives us hope. He will supply what we lack.

DAY 2: POSITIVE PEER PRESSURE

Peer pressure. Do you remember hearing warnings about the effects of peer pressure when you were a teenager? Choose your friends wisely. Be careful whom you hang out with. You will become like them.

The idea presented in Hebrews 10:24 is that we can *positively* influence others to care for one another.

We have been studying the past four weeks about how Jesus is better, and thus, why God is making us more like him. We've seen that one of the ways he does this is through other people and their examples.

1. There are several models in the Bible of people who supported each other in hard times and helped them persevere.

Verses	Who spurred on whom?	How?
Exodus 17:10-13		
Daniel 1:8, 11-13		
2 Timothy 1:2-7		

It is inspiring to read these stories in Scripture. Stirring up one another to love and good deeds looks different depending on the community.

At my last duty station, I attended a small group that met every other week. We studied various books of the Bible together, but we started each meeting by sharing our devotional time. It was incredibly encouraging to hear what God was teaching his people through his Word. Not everyone shared each week. There was no judgment if you remained quiet.

Instead of feeling shame for not sharing, I was hungry to find out what God was going to teach me the next week so I could come back and share with my friends. That is the kind of positive peer pressure Hebrews is talking about.

I've also been stirred up to love and good deeds by merely watching other believers live their lives. Observing a mom correct her child gently rather than yelling at them, spurs me on to be gentler with my children. Hearing another wife build up her husband in front of others reminds me I should do the same for my husband. Whether big or little, we can be the catalyst for growth in others' lives.

2. Can you think of a time when you were spurred to love and good deeds by someone else? Describe what happened.

Remember how we talked about being the body of Christ last week? This concept comes into play again here. As connected members, we need to stir up one another so that the body can work together as a healthy whole.

3. Read Ephesians 4:11-16. What is the purpose of each part of the body functioning properly?

Spiritual growth does not occur in a vacuum. We need each other. Let's resolve this week to live our lives in such a way that either explicitly or implicitly, we spur someone else on to love and good deeds.

DAY 3: BE AUTHENTIC

Authenticity. Transparency. Real. Raw. More and more, we see a desire for this in our culture. Perhaps it's a backlash against hypocrisy. Or maybe it's just a desire to stop hiding and embrace who we are. Matching what you say to what you do is a crucial part of integrity.

If we are going to be women who inspire others to love and good deeds, we have to be women who authentically live this out. To care in the ways Jesus did. Authentically.

1. Read Hebrews 13:1. Define brotherly love.

As believers, we are part of a family and should think of one another in this way. I admit this can be difficult at times, but think of the benefits. When we imagine ourselves as big sisters, modeling for our younger siblings how to act, the effect is remarkable. When we think of the love that exists inside a healthy family, we begin to see a picture of what God wants for us.

2. In what ways do you treat a family member differently than a stranger?

The remainder of Hebrews 13 illustrates how brotherly love can appear in the life of a believer.

3. Match the verses with their description of brotherly love.

Hebrews 13:2	Contentment
Hebrews 13:3	Hospitality
Hebrews 13:4	Healthy marriages
Hebrews 13:5	Imitation of mentors
Hebrews 13:7	Obedience
Hebrews 13:17	Prayer
Hebrews 13:18	Sharing in suffering

4. Look back over the list. Choose two and describe how each one illustrates brotherly love.

Now let's think about our own lives. Do we love authentically? Do we say we love others but neglect their needs? Do we envy what they have instead of rejoicing with them and being content with our lot? Are we welcoming and hospitable or closed off and distant?

Authentic love is hard. That's why we need to be surrounded by a community of believers to encourage us, provoke us, and remind us to trust in God. As much as we need to model these things for others, we need models ourselves. Only then can we persevere and continue to grow in our relationship with God.

5. Think about this past week. Who has modeled brotherly love to you? What did she or he do?

6. List three ways you can show brotherly love this week. Think of whom you can inspire in the process.

DAY 4: GOOD DEEDS

It's December while I'm writing, and it seems like everyone is thinking about good works. Whether it's because they're hoping to avoid coal in their stockings or garner the perfect gift, people are paying it forward in drive-through windows, setting out refreshments for delivery truck personnel, or donating to local food banks.

Good deeds are an integral part of every religion. Most assert that they pave the path to salvation. Christianity is different. Good works do nothing to gain favor with God. Jesus did it all. Of course, as Christians, we still perform good deeds. The difference is we do them out of love for God and gratitude for what he's done for us. Not because we're trying to earn our salvation.

> *For by grace you have been saved through faith. And this is not your own doing; it is the gift of God, not a result of works, so that no one may boast. For we are his workmanship, created in Christ Jesus for good works, which God prepared beforehand, that we should walk in them. —Ephesians 2:8-9*

According to these verses, what is the relationship between our salvation and good works? Who is the author of our good works?

Sometimes we forget what God has done. We default into wrong thinking and unbelief.

A community of believers reminds us who God is and what he has done, which corrects our thinking, and inspires us to believe—which then produces love and good works.

1. Write out Hebrews 10:24 below.

We've already talked about love, but it's worth mentioning that love leads the way in this verse. Without love, our good works are pointless (1 Corinthians 13:1-3). The Bible also tells us that good works done in love have a purpose.

2. Look up Matthew 5:14-16. When others see our good works, what will they do?

The good deeds we perform are not for our benefit. They are to bring glory to God and to lead others to faith in Him. This encourages us when we become weary. Loving others and performing good works can be exhausting. It requires sacrifice. But like Jesus, if we look to the joy set before us – the hope that something we do might bring someone else to Christ – we can continue giving of ourselves and serving those around us.

3. Brainstorm a list of good deeds you could perform in love this week. Then prayerfully choose one to implement.

DAY 5: DOING HARD THINGS TOGETHER

Recently I was browsing new room décor for my elementary-age daughter. She's growing up fast, and I want her room to be a safe place that is warm and inspiring. So, no matter where the military sends us, her space can be a haven.

I'm a sucker for anything with words on it: a wooden plaque, hand-lettered signs, scripted pillowcases. You get the idea. In my search, I came across this phrase – "beautiful girl, you can do hard things." It immediately resonated with me.

This military life is hard. The Christian life is hard. The author of Hebrews would not have written chapter 10, verses 24-25, if it weren't hard. "And let us consider how to stir up one another to love and good works, not neglecting to meet together, as is the habit of some, but encouraging one another, and all the more as you see the Day drawing near."

That phrase ("beautiful girl, you can do hard things") made me think of these verses. When it's hard to love. When it's hard to do something for someone else. We need reminders from the Word of God, from each other, that we can do hard things. Not because we're so great, but because we have the Holy Spirit residing inside us.

1. Look up John 14:15-17. What does Jesus say we will do if we love him?

Whom does he say he will ask God to give us?

The Holy Spirit is a gift from God to help us live this hard life, to serve others, to love when it hurts, to forgive, to sacrifice, to die to self. We are not alone.

We do not have to muster up the energy, seeking to obey God in our strength. We have a helper accessible any time we need him. And he's not just some half-wit secondary assistant. He is God himself!

The world tells us that we can do hard things, but the subtle message is that we can do it on our own. Especially if we have a sign hanging in our room that tells us we can. The Bible tells us the truth. A poster won't cut it.

We need Jesus.

2. How is it hard for you in your current circumstances to love others and perform good works? How can you rely on the Holy Spirit to help you obey in spite of the challenges?

Galatians 6:7-10 provides some encouragement when we are feeling weary.

> Do not be deceived: God is not mocked, for whatever one sows, that will he also reap. For the one who sows to his own flesh will from the flesh reap corruption, but the one who sows to the Spirit will from the Spirit reap eternal life. And let us not grow weary of doing good, for in due season we will reap, if we do not give up. So then, as we have opportunity, let us do good to everyone, and especially to those who are of the household of faith.

3. How do these verses encourage you not to give up?

God knows we will grow weary at times and will want to give up. But his grace is there to meet us through his word and his people. Beautiful girl, you can do hard things.

H2O: CHARITABLE ACTS*

When you do something for someone else out of love, you perform a charitable act. A kindness, a favor, a good work. It does not seek a reward or recognition. Good works can be elaborate or simple, costly or inexpensive, yet good works are infused with love.

Remember, the practice of charitable acts does not earn you more favor with God. The hope is that it will point others to God, bringing him glory, and provoke believers to love and good deeds in their own lives.

- Look at a calendar for your upcoming week.
- Think of some charitable deeds you can perform each day and write them in your calendar.
- Find ways to build good works into your daily routine.

*H20 stands for Habits to Outcome. Each week we will introduce a particular spiritual discipline to help you grow and better apply the concepts of this Bible study.

DIGGING DEEPER: CONNECTING WITH HEROES OF THE FAITH

Love, humility, and generosity are essential ingredients for relationships with others.

One of the greatest friendship stories in the Bible occurs in the Old Testament.

David and Jonathan had a special relationship. Jonathan was the son of King Saul, and presumably, the next in line for the throne. David was God's chosen vessel, destined to take over Saul's kingdom. Jonathan grew up in the palace; David grew up in sheep pastures. It was an unlikely pairing. Only God could have designed this combination.

> *As soon as he had finished speaking to Saul, the soul of Jonathan was knit to the soul of David, and Jonathan loved him as his own soul. And Saul took him that day and would not let him return to his father's house. Then Jonathan made a covenant with David, because he loved him as his own soul. And Jonathan stripped himself of the robe that was on him and gave it to David and his armor, and even his sword and his bow and his belt. —Samuel 18:1-4*

Jonathan gave David his robe, armor, and weapons as a sign of their deep friendship, and to dress him appropriately for the royal court like a prince and soldier rather than a shepherd.[22]

In his love for David, Jonathan humbled himself and gave generously to his friend. He no longer thought of himself as the crown prince but esteemed David higher than himself. This act inspired David and spurred him on to greatness (1 Samuel 18:5).

Not long after this, Jonathan's father became jealous of David and sought to kill him. Jonathan remained in contact with David and did whatever he could to help him (1 Samuel 20:4). Jonathan's loyalty to David never wavered, even when his father tried to kill him for it.

---

[22] https://biblehub.com/commentaries/gill/1_samuel/18.htm, accessed 12/6/19.

And let us not grow weary of doing good, for in due season we will reap, if we do not give up. So then, as we have opportunity, let us do good to everyone, and especially to those who are of the household of faith.

Galatians 6:9-10

WEEK SIX

Intentional Community

This is the final week. I can't believe it's almost over. I have so enjoyed meeting with you through the pages of this study each day. I hope you have enjoyed it too! My prayer is that when you close this book, you will be encouraged by the growth you've experienced in your relationship with God and with other people. I hope you will have an even deeper desire to build community with those around you.

Building Community

Building community - intentional community – is no easy task. Whether we wear a uniform or are married to one who does, we are busy people. We often lack the time, energy, or resources to find a Christian community in which we can be encouraged and, in turn, build others up.

According to Hebrews 10:24-25 we do not have a choice. "And let us consider how to stir up one another to love and good works, **not neglecting to meet together**, as is the habit of some, but encouraging one another, and all the more as you see the Day drawing near" (emphasis added).

We are not Lone Rangers

Theologians, pastors, and Bible study leaders often use these verses as a defense for church attendance. Many people, even back in New Testament times, questioned the necessity of church. There was already a trend towards "lone ranger Christianity." We see this even more today, and in the military, particularly.

Whether you're on a ship where only three people attend chapel or deployed to the Middle East where you can't get a Sunday off, it's easy to dismiss the idea altogether.

In our technology-saturated culture, we can stream live church services, download sermons and podcasts, and tell our devices to play worship music. What's the point of getting up early on a Sunday to go to church when we can access it right from the comfort of our homes?

Yet we receive so much more when we are part of a local body of believers. The church is people who can speak comfort when we are grieving, women who can bring a meal when we've just given birth, small groups to live life alongside us.

The Struggle of Finding a Faith Community

As a military wife myself, I know finding a church is difficult. There is no perfect church. In some duty stations, my place of worship is somewhere I go on Sundays, but it is not really where I find community. It's merely a place where I worship, hear God's word preached, serve where I can, and submit to their authority. I'm left to find community and deep relationships in other places such as a local women's Bible study, like Protestant Women of the Chapel. At some duty stations, I've found community, service, sound biblical teaching, and Christ-centered worship all in one place, but that's incredibly rare.

Regardless of choices at our current duty stations, we need to commit to a local body of believers. It's important to be intentional about attending, not in a legalistic way, but out of a desire to grow spiritually. Often God uses the not-so-good church to develop our character and perseverance.

This has been a relatively new concept for me. I used to go to church (or a local body of believers), and ask, "What can you do for me?" I was a consumer. I'm learning now that God has a much bigger picture in mind for his church. It's not just about me. The point of meeting together, as emphasized by the author of Hebrews, is to encourage and stir one another up to love and good works. We spent the past several weeks looking at how to do that.

Discipleship

Another word for stirring up one another to love and good deeds is discipleship. The concept of discipleship was close to Jesus's heart. In his final words to his disciples, he said,

"Go therefore and make disciples of all nations, baptizing them in the name of the Father and of the Son and of the Holy Spirit, **teaching them to observe all that I have commanded you**. And behold, I am with you always, to the end of the age" (Matthew 28:19-20, emphasis added).

Discipleship sounds like a massive, churchy word, but it just means what verse 20 explains—*teaching them to observe all that I have commanded you.*

As we build relationships with other believers, we teach each other how to walk as Jesus walked. This is how we grow together. This happens if we are intentional about it.

HOMEWORK

In your homework this week, we will tie it all together and notice the importance of community for our spiritual growth.

And let us consider how to stir up one another to love and good works, not neglecting to meet together as is the habit of some, but encouraging one another, and all the more as you see the Day drawing near. —Hebrews 10:24-25

DAY 1: JESUS' EXAMPLE OF INTENTIONAL COMMUNITY

As we saw in Week One, Jesus is our example. He's who we want to be when we grow up. The author of Hebrews reminds us of his identity.

Long ago, at many times and in many ways, God spoke to our fathers by the prophets, but in these last days he has spoken to us by his Son, whom he appointed the heir of all things, through whom also he created the world. He is the radiance of the glory of God and the exact imprint of his nature, and he upholds the universe by the word of his power. —Hebrews 1:1-3

Jesus shows us who God is. Through Jesus's life, we learn many things about God that were more difficult to see in the Old Testament. One of those is God's passion for the intentional community.

When Jesus began his earthly ministry, he did not go out alone. He went to other people and asked them to follow him.

1. Look up the following verses and record the names of those he chose and how he called them.

Verses	Names	Method
Matthew 4:18-22		
Matthew 9:9		
Luke 6:12-16		

Jesus was very intentional in his choice of people. He spent three years with them, pouring into them what he wanted them to know. Much of this he did through modeling.

2. According to the following verses, what are some things Jesus modeled to his disciples?

Matthew 6:9-13

Mark 6:30-33

Luke 9:10-17

3. Can you think of any more examples?

Jesus spent time with crowds. He spent time with his 12 disciples. But there were also times when Jesus took just two or three of his disciples with him. An entire Bible study could be written on how he intentionally organized his time!

When we look at his life and ministry, we see that he invested in relationships, in people's hearts. For three years, Jesus poured into a select few. As they learned from him, that select few poured into other people's lives and impacted the whole world for the gospel.
Before Jesus ascended to heaven after his resurrection, he told the disciples what would happen next.

4. Read Acts 1:8. Where would the disciples be witnesses?

God's plan is for his message to spread throughout the entire world, using people. Missionaries continue to travel to unreached people groups, telling others about God's love and his ultimate good deed (our salvation). While we may not be missionaries sent out from a church, the U.S. Government sends each one of us to all corners of the globe. We, too, can impact the world.

5. How can you intentionally build community in the place where God has sent you?

6. How does Jesus's model of pouring into a few people help you to form realistic goals for discipleship?

DAY 2: INTENTIONAL COMMUNITY AND SPIRITUAL DRIFTING

Shortly after my fourth PCS as an Army wife, I gave birth to my daughter. Moving in the middle of a pregnancy was difficult in many respects, but perhaps the most challenging thing for me was building relationships as a new mom. I was home so much more than I had been before, and since I had just moved, I didn't know anyone. I prioritized feeding and nap schedules over Bible study and church, and before I knew it, my relationship with God began to suffer.

I started to drift.

1. Have you ever had a similar experience? If so, describe what happened.

The author of Hebrews reminds us that an intentional community prevents drifting.

2. How do you see that reflected in Hebrews 10:24-25?

As Christians, we can drift in many ways. Because we are still sinners, we tend to get things wrong and revert to incorrect thinking. We see this in the Bible repeatedly. But what we also see is how God uses other people to get us back on track.

3. Look up Galatians 2:11-14. Describe what happens.

Paul's confrontation is a clear picture of why we need other people in our lives to keep us from drifting. Peter (Cephas) was changing his stance depending on which group he associated with rather than standing firm on the truth of the gospel.

We need to be close enough to other people that we can see when they are drifting. Not to judge them but to encourage them to make a mid-course correction.

4. In what ways can you help other women when you see drift in their lives?

When I was drifting, no one around me knew it. My husband was deployed. I lived far away from my family, and I didn't have any friends. I finally had enough of the loneliness and decided to do something. I hired a babysitter, so I didn't have to sacrifice my daughter's naps while I went to Bible study. There, I found my community.

Thankfully no one corrected me as sharply as Paul corrected Peter. Somehow it was enough just being around other believers again, worshipping with them, and hearing them talk about the Bible. Their examples encouraged me to think beyond my tiny world and once again pursue a closer walk with Jesus.

God used a community of believers
to correct my course.

5. Do you see drift in your own life? What relationships do you need to build or maintain (or avoid) to protect yourself from drift?

DAY 3: INTENTIONAL COMMUNITY
AND HOLDING FAST

There are times in military life when we are more vulnerable—moves, deployments, promotions (or lack of), toxic commands, transitions, etc. All of these and more present us with a choice – to drift or to stay the course. We are always moving closer to God or further away from him.

1. Evaluate where you are currently. Are you closer to God than you were this time last year or further away?

Relationships with other believers can help us grow closer to God. It's sort of like when we're working out. Whether it's PT or a class at the gym, other people push us to do better. If we work out on our own, we might cut corners and finish early. The people around us help us stick to the course and finish well. They push us beyond what we think we can handle.

We've already talked briefly about the relationship between Paul and Timothy. Paul was a seasoned missionary mentoring a younger, inexperienced Timothy as he established a church. There are two letters from Paul to Timothy in the New Testament. They're full of warnings, encouragement, and leadership development.

2. Choose three of the following passages and describe how Paul inspires Timothy to hold fast to his faith, to stay the course.

1 Timothy 1:18-19

1 Timothy 4:11-16

1 Timothy 6:20-21

2 Timothy 1:6-7

2 Timothy 2:1-2

2 Timothy 3:14-17

Although Timothy grew up learning about the faith, he too struggled when hard times hit. Just as he needed someone to remind him of truth, to continue to fight for what's right, and to persevere regardless of difficulty, so also we need people who can encourage us to hold fast. Conversely, we need to help others endure the challenges they face.

3. List two ways you can encourage a specific person to hold fast to their faith and persevere.

4. Do you have someone in your life like Paul? Someone who reminds you of what's right, gives you the courage to keep going, and prompts you to use what God has given you? If so, write them a note of thanks for all they do to encourage you.
If you don't have someone like that in your life, ask God to send someone.

DAY 4: INTENTIONAL COMMUNITY AND ENCOURAGEMENT

Have you ever noticed how some people are naturally gifted in certain areas?

One of my friends is a natural encourager. With her words and actions – even her expressions - she lights up the room. People leave her presence feeling lighter, happier, and more confident. I am so grateful for her! But unfortunately, encouraging others does not come naturally to me. It's something I'm asking God to develop in me.

1. Where do you fit on the encourager scale? How often do you encourage others?

Always   Often   Sometimes   Never

I don't know how intentional my friend is with encouragement. It could be what looks effortless to me is gained by prayer, purpose, and intentionality.

I have other friends who never seem to meet a stranger. Wherever they go, they know at least five people. For me – the introvert – I have to remind myself of God's plan for relationships and community before I step out to join one. I have to remember that it's for my good and the good of others.

Joining or forming a community of believers is the first step. But the second step, according to Hebrews, is what we do in that community.

And let us consider how to stir up one another to love and good works, not neglecting to meet together, as is the habit of some, but encouraging one another, and all the more as you see the Day drawing near. —Hebrews 10:24-25

2. Read Ephesians 4:29. How are we to build up others in the community?

When I read "corrupting talk" I think of bad language, but it can also be discouraging words. This verse reminds me of the alternative – to choose my words wisely, to think of what fits the situation, and then to build my friends up accordingly. This does not come naturally, at least to me. It requires intentionality.

3. Read the story of Moses encouraging Joshua in Deuteronomy 31:7-8. How do you think Joshua felt after hearing these words?

Imagine for a moment that Moses didn't say those things. Imagine that he used discouraging, corrupting words. What might that have looked like? How would Joshua have felt?

We often don't realize the power our words hold. We might sometimes recognize the damage they cause, but do we consider the power they can give someone? When we build others up, we help that person see themselves as God sees them. Recognizing their potential and calling it out gives individuals the courage they need to do what God has called them to do. We can make heroes out of people by merely opening our mouths and speaking a word of kindness and encouragement.

4. Think of someone you can encourage this week and write down one specific way to do it. Use Ephesians 4:29 as a guide.

DAY 5: GROWING TOGETHER

The military culture is one of initiation and leadership. If we aren't finding what we need, we go out and get it. So it is with community. We can't be women who wait for people to come to us. We need to build community wherever we find ourselves.

One way to intentionally seek out others is to look for someone who has what you lack. For example, if you don't know how to pray, listen to how other people speak to God. When you hear someone who prays the way you want to pray, ask that person to teach you. Or if you desire to be more generous, find someone who excels in that area and figure out ways to be around her.

I know of one woman who tried to memorize Scripture. She knew someone in her church who remembered hundreds of verses, but she wasn't sure how to approach her. When she finally called and asked, the woman said, "What time does your son nap?" The next week she came over during naptime and began to show her how to memorize the Bible. Sometimes all we have to do is ask!

1. What is something you aspire to do or have, spiritually speaking? Who can you intentionally seek out to help you develop this skill?

An influencer said, "We're emboldened when surrounded by people who tell us we're AMAZING and CAPABLE, but we endure and persevere when surrounded by people who tell us that CHRIST IS MUCH MORE SO."[23]

This resonated with me deeply. I love having people around me who tell me how awesome I am, but when I'm struggling, that can sometimes feel empty. But to have someone tell me that Jesus is incredible and will help me get through whatever it is I'm going through – that's not empty. It's life-giving.

---

[23] https://www.instagram.com/p/B6CHcBfgnE_/?igshid=ux5jo925xpyw, accessed 12/16/19.

Perhaps you're in a season where you have challenging people in your life. Could it be that God is calling you to be the influencer? I think we often doubt ourselves and wonder if we have what it takes.

2. How does 2 Peter 1:3-4 speak to this?

God gives us what we need. When we were children, we were on the receiving end of things. Then there was a subtle shift through adolescence as we gained more and more responsibilities. Eventually, we grew into adults who can impact the next generation. Our Christian growth is similar. Early on, we have to learn so much; we don't do a lot of giving. But as we mature, a shift occurs. Soon we begin teaching others.

3. "When I was a child, I spoke like a child, I thought like a child, I reasoned like a child. When I became a man, I gave up childish ways" (1 Corinthians 13:11).
How do you need to give up childish ways and begin to pour into other people, rather than merely receiving what others have to offer?

Sometimes teaching someone else is the best way to grow.

We won't be like Jesus until we get to heaven. It's a long path towards completion. But we can persevere if we build communities that inspire us, hold us accountable, and give us opportunities to share what we've learned. And just maybe, our community will spread to other places—and the hope Jesus brings will multiply through the entire world, one military woman at a time.

H2O: SILENCE AND SOLITUDE*

Our world is loud, literally and figuratively. We are surrounded by noise whether it's from our environment or the constant input of the digital age. If we are going to be women who intentionally build biblical community, we will need times of silence and solitude. These quiet moments will provide clarity and refreshment as we seek to pour into others. Jesus knew this and practiced it himself.

> *And after he had dismissed the crowds, he up on a mountain by himself to pray. When evening came, he was there alone. —Matthew 14:23*

> *And rising very early in the morning, while it was still dark, he departed and went out to a desolate place, and there he prayed. —Mark 1:35*

> *In these days he went out to the mountain to pray, and all night he continued in prayer to God. —Luke 6:12*

If Jesus practiced silence and solitude, how much more should we?

Find some pockets of time this week when you can get away by yourself to be quiet. Whether it's early in the morning, late at night, or while hiding in the bathroom in the middle of the day, look for those moments. Practice being alone and quiet before God. Reflect on his character traits. Talk to him. Rest in him.

*H2O stands for Habits to Outcome. Each week we will introduce a particular spiritual discipline to help you grow and better apply the concepts of this Bible study.

DIGGING DEEPER: CONNECTING WITH HEROES OF THE FAITH

There's been much talk lately about the lack of community in our highly individualistic, tech-savvy culture. Women especially seem to memorialize the "good ole' days" when our ancestors went to the river to wash their clothes, solve the world's problems and went home better equipped to handle the frustrations of family life.

In biblical times, the community seemed to develop in a similar, more natural way. The culture predisposed itself to living together, eating together, and worshiping together. But there was also an intentional component to this.

In Acts 2:42-47 we see a picture of the New Testament church:

> And they **devoted** themselves to the apostles' teaching and the fellowship, to the breaking of bread and the prayers. And awe came upon every soul, and many wonders and signs were being done through the apostles. And all who believed were together and had all things in common. And they were selling their possessions and belongings and distributing the proceeds to all, as any had need. And day by day, attending the temple together and baking bread in their homes, they received their food with glad and generous hearts, praising God and having favor with all the people. And the Lord added to their number day by day those who were being saved. (emphasis added)

This group of people was serious about growing in their faith. They intentionally chose to center their lives on God and one another. Notice too that they didn't spend all their time together at the temple. Much of it was spent in each other's homes, doing ordinary, mundane tasks – cooking, eating, and celebrating.

We can learn from their example by choosing to center our lives on these same priorities: God and each other. As we bring people into our lives, letting them see how we eat, shop, correct our kids, deal with leave paperwork, and clean our spaces, we can also teach them how to love God in the midst.

Again, this will require intentionality on our part, just as it did for the early Christians. Our bodies will die but our souls will live on forever. Doesn't it make sense then that we spend our time investing there—in other's souls!

CONCLUSION

Writing this Bible study has caused me to grow in ways I never could have imagined. When I was first asked to write, I thought there was no way I could do it. There were a lot of things circulating in my corner of the world, and I already felt overwhelmed. How could I add one more thing? I prayed about it, and God asked me two questions:

- Do you depend on me?
- Will this cause you to depend on me more?

While I thought I depended on God, I realized that in actuality, I sought to control my life in just the right ways so I didn't need God too much. I definitely needed him for the big things – like forgiveness, salvation, and eternal security.

But did I need him in the small things—like controlling my anger when I'm overtired, speaking gently to my kids when I felt the stress of a deadline, or putting my husband first when all I wanted was to do something for myself?

I knew when I said yes to writing this Bible study, I was saying yes to a life that depended on God in deeper, more profound ways. But I had no idea just how deep he would take me.

My prayer for you is that God has taken you deeper through this study, challenging you to grow in your understanding of who he is. Now more than ever, I believe that studying God's character is a key element of our spiritual growth. I hope you have found comfort and encouragement in learning about him these past six weeks.

And as we tackled the concepts of drifting and holding fast, I hope you found some practical ideas to stay the course and help others do the same. The military lifestyle is fast-paced. If we're not careful, we'll get swept up in a current that takes us further from our Father. We need the truth of Scripture and encouragement from others to keep us afloat.

In those final weeks of exploring love, good deeds, and intentional community, I pray you discovered tools to build communities deliberately focused on discipleship and building others up. There is no doubt that God loves to use ordinary people for extraordinary purposes. As we faithfully walk with him and teach others to do the same, we acquire a front-row seat to God's most miraculous work - turning hearts and minds back to himself.

Though this study has ended, we will never stop growing. God will find new ways to teach us, challenge us, improve us, and transform us from one degree of glory to another. May this study be a small step in your transformation process. I assure you it has been a huge step in mine.

And we all, with unveiled face, beholding the glory of the Lord, are being transformed into the same image from one degree of glory to another. For this comes from the Lord who is the Spirit. 2 Corinthians 3:18

APPENDIX A
Facilitator's Guide

GROWING TOGETHER – LEADER'S GUIDE

We designed the following pages to support and encourage small group leaders or facilitators of this study. This appendix includes what to do before your group meets the first time, a sample timeline for a one-hour discussion, general information about the format of the study, and some warnings and helps for sections of the study that might touch tender places for participants.

The weeks of this guide correspond with the weeks of the study. Facilitator's Guide notes should be read the week prior to the lesson, so you will have time to make any necessary preparations for your group time.

If you are leading a group study, please feel free to reach out to Planting Roots using a contact from our website or any of our social media platforms. We would love to connect and support your study any way we can, particularly through prayer.

What to Do Before Your First Meeting

1. Pray for God to give you his wisdom and discernment as you lead women through the study.
2. Ask someone to pray for you during your time as a group leader.
3. Be sure you have good contact information for each of your participants.
4. Contact them before the first group meeting and see if they have any questions.
5. Read through this Facilitator's Guide so you are familiar with how the lessons will flow.
6. Dedicate a notebook to use as a group prayer journal during your time together.

7. Consider a small welcome gift for the ladies. Perhaps print outs of the downloadable content available at **plantingroots.net** on card stock, some pens, sticky notes, chocolates, etc.

8. Either provide or suggest the ladies purchase a journal or notebook to record what God teaches them throughout the study.

9. Take a look at the space where you'll be meeting and consider ways to make it comfortable and functional for your participants.

10. Consider your timeline for completing the study. If you have a limited number of meeting dates or schedule conflicts, you will need to combine lessons.

General Information

Each meeting of this six-week includes a lesson to help participants focus on a small portion of the text at a time. Throughout the lesson, we have included some reflection questions to process key concepts or thought patterns. Each week has five days of homework. The questions in the lesson and homework assignments serve as your material for discussion during class. Keep in mind that you may not have time to cover them all. As you pray for your class and your lesson each week, highlight or mark the questions the Holy Spirit prompts you to be sure to discuss. Ask your participants if they had a question they particularly wanted to discuss or one they didn't understand.

As a facilitator, it isn't your job to know all the answers. That's God's job. It is acceptable to say you don't know and then seek a study resource, mentor, chaplain, or pastor to help you learn the answer before the next meeting.

Consider some of the following for your first group meeting.

- Be sure to discuss the best way to communicate with each participant as they sign up for the group.

- Pass around the journal at the beginning of class and ask ladies to write down their requests or praises. Ask them to indicate if their request is personal and they would rather not have it shared with the entire group by clearly placing a "P" next to their entry.

- Ask for a volunteer to serve as a group admin to assist with distribution of prayer requests and weekly contacts.

- Consider establishing a Facebook group or other group messaging system to keep your participants connected throughout the week.

- Begin and end each class on time.

- Don't be afraid of silence. Give participants time to chime in before you tell them all the answers. Pay attention to who does most of the talking and invite those who are quieter to share their insights as well.

Sample Timeline

0900 – Open with prayer. Pass around the prayer journal.

0905 – Welcome the ladies to the Bible study.

Share 2-3 things you would like the ladies to know about yourself. Allow the ladies to share their name and one thing about themselves or another icebreaker in later weeks.

0915 – Give a brief summary of the week's lesson.

0920 – Share what impacted you most during the week's lesson. Hit the highlights that spoke to your heart.

0925 – Ask the ladies to share what impacted them.

0935 – Use chapter questions or homework to guide the discussion. Prioritize questions you'd like to cover as you work through each week's lesson. You know your group, so feel free to pick and choose the questions that would be most relevant.

0950 - Take time to point out areas of life application and allow the ladies to speak to this as well. If time is short as you dig into the life application questions, encourage the ladies to answer them in their journals.

1000 – Close your Bible study time in prayer. If you're comfortable and it is appropriate to the group dynamics, include the requests ladies wrote in the journal.

Guide outline

- Lesson summary in 3-4 sentences
- Life application suggestion
- Suggested questions for the homework to cover
- Journal prompts
- Prayer prompts
- Word study/scripture memory
-

WEEK 1 – I WANT TO BE LIKE JESUS WHEN I GROW UP

LESSON SUMMARY

Living in a military community can be rough at times. There are challenges that are unique to us alone. This week's study will take you into the depths of who Jesus is and how knowing him completely can change everything.

LIFE APPLICATION QUESTION

In light of the following verse and all you have discovered this week, how will you apply this truth to your everyday life? "He is the radiance of the glory of God and the exact imprint of his nature, and he upholds the universe by the word of his power. After making purification for sins, he sat down at the right hand of the Majesty on high" (Hebrews 1:3 ESV).

Example: "Working through the homework this week helped me understand who Jesus truly is. I plan to make scripture prayer cards and place them throughout our home to help me memorize the verses and recite them when I become anxious."

SUGGESTED QUESTIONS FROM THE HOMEWORK

1. Compare Hebrews 1:3 with Colossians 1:15-17. What did you learn about Jesus? (Day 1)

2. Read Hebrews 1:10-12. What is changing in your life right now? How can God's immutability bring you comfort? (Day 2)

3. Look up Hebrews 4:14-16. How does knowing that Jesus can sympathize with you encourage you? (Day 4)

4. Saul (later, Paul) had a dramatic encounter with Jesus that turned his life upside down. In what ways has Jesus already turned your life upside down? How will focusing on his attributes continue to change you?

SCRIPTURE MEMORY

"And we know that for those who love God all things work together for good, for those who are called according to his purpose. For those whom he foreknew he predestined to be conformed to the image of his Son, in order that he might be the firstborn among many brothers. —Romans 8:28-29

PRAYER PROMPTS

Encourage the ladies to pray the Lord's Prayer as a closing for your time together. 'Our Father in heaven, hallowed be your name. Your kingdom come, your will be done, on earth as it is in heaven. Give us this day our daily bread, and forgive us our debts, as we also have forgiven our debtors. And lead us not into temptation, but deliver us from evil" (Matthew 6:9-13).

H2O

Encourage your ladies with the following scripture to take the H2O challenge to heart and begin to commit to a daily time spent in the Word and prayer. "Therefore, holy brothers, you who share in a heavenly calling, consider Jesus, the apostle and high priest of our confession" (Hebrews 3:1).

CAUTIONS/SUGGESTIONS

Remember that there might be ladies present who do not have a personal relationship with Christ. There might also be some who have a beginning faith, as well as some with a deeper faith. Be aware of this as you enter into discussions, prayer requests, and homework answers.

WEEK 2 – DANGERS OF DRIFTING

LESSON SUMMARY

We face many challenges in our military lifestyle—some we have no control over. We can often find ourselves at the mercy of others. In this week's lesson we find that we have a secure Savior who has promised to care for us in all situations. We can trust Jesus.

LIFE APPLICATION QUESTION

Identify the areas in your life where you are drifting. Now apply a scripture from this week's lesson to help aid you in refocusing your life course.

Example: "Iron sharpens iron, and one man sharpens another" (Proverbs 27:17). I often find myself hiding inside my home. This verse will remind me that I am a part of a Christian community and we need one another to grow and mature in our faith walk. I plan to add this verse to my scripture prayer cards."

SUGGESTED QUESTIONS FROM THE HOMEWORK

1. What does Ephesians 5:15-16 say about our time? How can we guard against distractions? (Day 1)

2. "Iron sharpens iron, and one man sharpens another" (Proverbs 27:17). How does community with others protect us from drifting? What are some ways someone else has sharpened you spiritually? In what ways can you sharpen another believer? (Day 3)

3. In what ways does a firm sense of identity guard against drifting? What are some ways you can remember your identity as a believer? How would your thoughts and behaviors change if you always remembered you are God's child? (Day 5)

4. Hard things happen to us. How does the story of Naomi, Ruth, and Boaz encourage you to not give up hope during difficult days?

SCRIPTURE MEMORY

Therefore we must pay much closer attention to what we have heard, lest we drift away from it. —
Hebrews 2:1

PRAYER PROMPTS

Using the following scripture, write a short prayer expressing your confidence in
God to guide you and rescue you when needed.

Example: "Jesus Christ is the same yesterday, today and forever" (Hebrews13:8).

Lord, thank you for the gift of salvation, the ministry of the Holy Spirit, and the
faithful love of like-minded believers. Help me to trust you with my soul, surrender
my heart to your will and allow other believers to speak into my life. I am so thankful
I do not have to do this on my own. In Jesus' name. Amen.

H2O

Take some time this week to journal your way through the Beatitudes found in
Matthew 5:2-10. It is a great reminder of how powerful the faith community can
become in your everyday life. We need one another.

CAUTIONS/SUGGESTIONS

Be mindful again of the different levels of faith that may be present within your
group of ladies. Make sure to guide the discussion according to what the Bible says
and not just thoughts, ideas and suppositions. We have unpacked a great deal of
truth this week, and it may bring many questions about their life application of
scripture. Remember to guide them back to the Word of God.

WEEK 3 – HOLDING FAST IN THE STORMS OF LIFE

LESSON SUMMARY

Trouble is coming. It always does. But we have a God who has already made a way of escape. We are halfway through our journey of "growing together" in our faith walk. This week we will blend who we know Jesus to be with what we can do to take ahold of that truth and thrive through our storms.

LIFE APPLICATION QUESTION

What are some of the things you hold fast to? Are they in accordance with the word of God? If not, what do you need to change? How can the truth of God's word help you change? What are you going to do different since you have encountered the truth of holding fast?

SUGGESTED FOUR QUESTIONS FROM THE HOMEWORK

1. Read aloud Exodus 34:6-7. How does God describe himself? In what way do these traits enable us to hold fast to God? (Day 1)

2. What situation is currently making it difficult for you to trust God? (Day 2)

3. Read Hebrews 3:12-13. How can other people help us hold fast to God? (Day 5)

4. Read Genesis 50:21. How does knowing that God brings good out of evil help you to hold fast as Joseph did?

SCRIPTURE MEMORY

Not only that, but we rejoice in our sufferings, knowing that suffering produces endurance, and endurance produces character, and character produces hope, and hope does not put us to shame, because God's love has been poured out into our hearts through the Holy Spirit who has been given to us. —Romans 5:3-5

PRAYER PROMPTS

Lord, help me to see you in all my everyday circumstances and choose to hold fast to your truth and not to what I think is right. In Jesus' name. Amen.
Share the plan of salvation with your ladies. Ask those who do not know Christ if they would like to accept him as their savior. "For God so loved the world, that he gave his only Son, that whoever believes in him should not perish but have eternal life" (John 3:16). For more information, see Appendix E.

H2O

Encourage your ladies to consider this scripture and write a heart prayer to the Lord in their journal this week. "But when Christ had offered for all time a single sacrifice for sins, he sat down at the right hand of God, waiting from that time until his enemies should be made a footstool for his feet" (Hebrews 10:12-13).

Example: Lord, your Word says that you sit at the right hand of God in power. I surrender to your perfect love and I will not walk in fear any longer. In Jesus' name. Amen.

CAUTIONS/SUGGESTIONS

Sharing the plan of salvation may lead to some of your ladies asking more in-depth questions and requesting a private prayer time. Ask some ladies ahead of time if they are willing to stay a bit after study to assist with prayer and questions. Take time to answer questions, and have other ladies on hand to pray with you one-on-one if necessary.

WEEK 4 – ENCOURAGEMENT

LESSON SUMMARY

We have a super power! It's encouragement. We who name the name of Jesus have a duty and a responsibility to help one another. Specifically, in the military community we are only as strong as the woman next to us. This week we will discover this super power, together!

LIFE APPLICATION QUESTION

Use the following verse to write a 3-step plan of how you would offer encouragement to someone: "That their hearts may be encouraged, being knit together in love, to reach all the riches of full assurance of understanding and the knowledge of God's mystery, which is Christ" (Colossians 2:2).

Example: 1) Commit to pray for my friend everyday. 2) Commit to sending a card, text or email with encouraging scriptures. 3) Invite my friend to get together and listen intentionally.

SUGGESTED QUESTIONS FROM THE HOMEWORK

1. Read Hebrews 10:19-25. How does believing verses 19-21 enable you to act out verses 22-25? (Day 1)

2. What are some ways you can encourage those around you to have greater confidence in God and boldly live out their faith? (Day 4)

3. Look up Romans 1:11-12. How have you been encouraged by someone else's faith? What are some ways you can stir up another believer's faith? (Day 5)

4. How does Barnabas's example inspire you to be an encourager when times are hard?

SCRIPTURE MEMORY

For I long to see you, that I may impart to you some spiritual gift to strengthen you – that is, that we may be mutually encouraged by each other's faith, both yours and mine. —Romans 1:11-12

PRAYER PROMPTS

Ask your ladies to pray silently through the following verses and record their thoughts in their journals. "Let no corrupting talk come out of your mouths, but only such as is good for building up, as fits the occasion, that it may give grace to those who hear" (Ephesians 4:29). "By this all people will know that you are my disciples, if you have love for one another" (John 13:35).

H2O

Encourage your ladies to record and meditate on the following verses in their journal: "And let us consider how to stir up one another to love and good works, not neglecting to meet together, as is the habit of some, but encouraging one another, and all the more as you see the Day drawing near" (Hebrews 10:24-25).

Allow the Holy Spirit to speak to them in regard to how they encourage others and how they allow others to encourage them. Ask if they are willing to share the thoughts that come to mind after listening to the Lord.

CAUTIONS/SUGGESTIONS

You are past the halfway mark of the study. Do not be discouraged if you have lost a few ladies along the way. This would be a great week to send them a personal email inviting them to finish strong. Also, some of your ladies may not have dug in quite as deep as others. Be sure to ask if anyone is struggling with the content.

WEEK 5 – LOVE AND GOOD WORKS

LESSON SUMMARY

Melissa, the author of our Bible study, hits the nail on the head with this statement: "Sometimes I wish there were parts of the Bible with a parenthetical statement that reads, 'does not apply to the military'." As we move towards the close of this Bible study, we will focus on love and how it absolutely changes us. Loving like Jesus within the military lifestyle is no easy task. It's hard.

LIFE APPLICATION QUESTION

How would this verse bear out in your everyday life? *"And let us consider how to stir up one another to love and good works"* (Hebrews 10:24).

Example: Today I spent the morning with my daughter as we did our quiet time together. We are using our meal times to talk about what God is doing in her life.

SUGGESTED FOUR QUESTIONS FROM THE HOMEWORK

1. Note how Jesus showed love to others in the following passages: John 13:1-15, Matthew 4:14, and Mark 6:34. In what ways do you need to grow to be more like Jesus in this area of loving others? (Day 1)

2. How does Ephesians 2:8-10 describe the relationship between good works and salvation? Who is the author of good works? Why does that matter? (Day 4)

3. Read John 14:15-17. What does it look like to rely on the Holy Spirit for help to love when it's hard? (Day 5)

4. In what ways did Jonathan humble himself to love David? How does this inspire you to humility as you love and perform good works?

SCRIPTURE MEMORY

And let us consider how to stir up one another to love and good works, not neglecting to meet together, as is the habit of some, but encouraging one another, and all the more as you see the Day drawing near. —Hebrews 10:24-25

PRAYER PROMPTS

Lord, your Word has declared that we are to love like Jesus does. He gave his life for us while we were yet sinners. Help us love like Jesus. Father, as we seek to love the unlovable, allow us to see them through your eyes, lost and in need of Jesus. Soften our hearts so that we may do good deeds in your name, drawing others to you. In Jesus Name, amen.

H2O

Remind your ladies to continue in the good works towards others for the sake of Christ. Share what you were able to accomplish this week as an encouragement for those who may have not embraced the H2O for this week.

CAUTIONS/SUGGESTIONS

There is one more week of study. Make sure you have been able to connect with each lady in your group. Begin to talk with them about their "next" Bible study.

WEEK 6 – INTENTIONAL COMMUNITY

LESSON SUMMARY

We wrap up this study with a keen awareness that Jesus is the best, and we are in need of community in order to thrive in our Christian walk. This week will guide us into a deeper understanding of what it means to grow together. We need one another, and God has already made provision for this through our faith communities.

LIFE APPLICATION QUESTION

Have you identified your faith community? What obstacles in your life right now are keeping you from thriving in a community?

SUGGESTED FOUR QUESTIONS FROM THE HOMEWORK

1. Look up Acts 1:8. Where did Jesus say his disciples would be witnesses? How can we intentionally build community (and thus, be Jesus's witnesses) right where we are? (Day 1)

2. Read through the passages in 1 and 2 Timothy in which Paul encourages Timothy to hold fast to his faith. In what ways can you intentionally do this for someone else? (Day 3)

3. Look up Ephesians 4:29. How are we to intentionally build up others in the community? (Day 4)

4. How does the Acts 2:42-47 example inspire you to bring people into your everyday life in order to teach them about God?

SCRIPTURE MEMORY

Go therefore and make disciples of all nations, baptizing them in the name of the Father and of the Son and of the Holy Spirit, teaching them to observe all that I have commanded you. And behold, I am with you always, to the end of the age. —Matthew 28:19-20

PRAYER PROMPTS

Allow your ladies to offer up prayers of thanksgiving for all they have learned during the course of the study.

H2O

Continue to spend time with the Lord even though this study has come to an end. Make a plan to build community where you are. Here are a couple suggestions: 1) Invite one of the ladies from this study to get together outside of class. Talk about how God has used the study to grow you in your faith walk. 2) Continue on with another study with the same ladies, or form a new group. 3) Share what you have learned with others.

CAUTIONS/SUGGESTIONS

You did it! Thank you for answering the call to lead! Encourage your ladies to continue with Bible study on their own and within a faith community. Ask if any of them need help finding a church home or a small group to continue to grow in faith.

APPENDIX B
How to Read the Bible for Personal Study

Let the word of Christ dwell in you richly, teaching and admonishing one another in all wisdom. —Colossians 3:16a

---

Studying the Bible for personal use is life changing! We are lifelong learners, and we are transformed by what we learn when we read God's word. We can study the Bible in a group or alone in our quarters. We study the Bible to get answers, gain guidance, avoid wrong teaching, and to know God. Reading the Bible increases our spiritual awareness. Our approach to the Bible matters:

- **Approach the Bible in prayer.** Ask the Holy Spirit to use God's Word to transform you.

- **Approach the Bible with expectancy.** Expect to encounter God in his living word.

- **Approach the Bible carefully.** Read verses in context, asking who, what, and why.

- **Approach the Bible thoughtfully.** Consider using a paper and pen for reflection.

Where to Start: If you're not using a study guide like this one, starting with the New Testament can be helpful. Afterwards, cycle back to the Old Testament to get a bigger picture. Try reading Bible books from the beginning—even just a chapter at a time—for context. As you read, ask yourself the following questions:

1. What do I learn about God?

2. How should I respond?

When to Read the Bible: You can read the Bible anytime! Many people like to read the Bible first thing in the morning to frame their day. You don't have to read the Bible just once a day either. Anytime you have a few moments for reflection and meditation, the Bible is great inspiration—especially Psalms and Proverbs. Lighter duty days and weekends can be good times for extended study or longer readings.

Study Aids: Many good "study" Bibles have comments and explanations. Consider reading the Scripture first before turning to the notes. This method allows you to discern the truth firsthand. A good study Bible gives some background on each book and tells who wrote it, when and why. If you have questions or concerns, find a solid Bible teacher, chaplain or Christian friend to help you. The Lord has gifted teachers who correctly understand and obey the truth. A good teacher, like a good drill sergeant, helps us learn the right way to keep in step.

Bottom Line: Approach the Bible prayerfully and humbly for a deeper understanding. Study verses in context and seek explanations from mature, seasoned Christians.

APPENDIX C
How to Memorize Scripture

I have stored up your word in my heart. —Psalm 119:11a

God's word is foundational to our spiritual maturity. Storing God's word in our heart means we have the truth whenever and wherever we need it. We do this by memorizing key and essential verses. Memorization allows Scripture to "take root."

Our generation has more information at our fingertips than any generation ever. Our smartphones, iPads and personal computers are readily available. Technically, we don't have to memorize anything. Even the latest SOP (Standard Operating Procedure) for the unit is available at our fingertips.

Still, memorizing information, especially Holy Scripture, is essential. Smartphones break, iPads lose energy, and we can't carry our computer on our back. We must remember important information. A pilot can't always fly on autopilot. I understand it's not easy. Our memory muscles need development. But the more we use our memory muscle, the stronger it gets.

Tips for Memorizing Scripture:

- Find a quiet place, free from distractions.

- Read the verse(s) at least 3X: first for the eyes, second for the mind, third for the heart.

- Say the verse out loud—speak it with understanding.

- Write it down. Carry it with you and refer to it during down times (in line, etc.).

- Read the passage at night before lights out. You will be amazed what your mind does while you are sleeping! You may awake with the words on your tongue!

As we know in the military, memorization can be a little frustrating at first. But the rewards are remarkable. Take your time. Remember how hard it was to memorize everyone's rank? Now you can recall ranks without a second thought.

Memorizing helps us capture each word and remember it in the future. Being involved with the verse makes memorization easier. Other methods of memorization, such as using music, might help you. Use hand signals or, if you're able, translate the verse into a different language. Repetition is important.

The goal is to let God's Word get deep into the recesses of your heart. Having a memorized verse spring up at just the right moment is encouraging and life changing!

APPENDIX D
How to Pray

And he (Jesus) told them a parable to the effect that they ought always to pray and not lose heart. —Luke 18:1

When we pray, we reach out to God. In the reaching, our attitude and spiritual awareness are revolutionized. Prayer is not some magical formula to get the right results. God is not a magician. Prayer is a relationship. God desires real and personal communication with us. He's more interested in what concerns us than how we pray. Prayer is personal.

In Matthew 6:9-13—called the Lord's Prayer—Jesus taught his disciples to pray. Many people use this as a pattern for prayer, and others use it as a daily prayer. Some do both!

> *Pray then like this: "Our Father in heaven, hallowed be your name. Your kingdom come, your will be done, on earth as it is in heaven. Give us this day our daily bread, and forgive us our debts, as we also have forgiven our debtors. And lead us not into temptation, but deliver us from evil. —Matthew 6:9-13*

The book of Psalms is full of beautiful prayers. We can pray these back to God, or we can speak to him and praise him freely and personally. Though we can (and should) pray anywhere, Jesus often took extended periods of time and went to solitary places to pray. What should we pray about? The book of Philippians gives us some clues:

> *The Lord is at hand; do not be anxious about anything, but in everything by prayer and supplication with thanksgiving let your requests be made known to God. And the peace of God which surpasses all understanding will guard your hearts and minds in Christ Jesus. —Philippians 4:5b-7*

When you pray, remember this:

- **Draw near to God and he will draw near to you** (James 4:8). Prayer is personal!

- **Pray about everything.** There are no secrets with the all-knowing God.

- **Pray with confidence.** God is not judging the delivery of your prayers!

- **Pray with thankfulness.** Gratitude is one of the ways God guards our hearts.

  Thus says the LORD who made the earth, the LORD who formed it to establish it – the LORD is His name: "Call to Me and I will answer you, and will tell you great and hidden things that you have not known. —Jeremiah 33:2-3

APPENDIX E
What Does It Mean to Be a Christian?

"Sirs, what must I do to be saved?" And they said, "Believe in the Lord Jesus, and you will be saved..." And he rejoiced along with his entire household that he had believed in God. —Acts 16:29-30, 34

What does it mean to be a Christian? It means believing in the Lord Jesus for salvation. In John 20:28, Thomas responds to Jesus saying, "My Lord and My God." Believing Christ is God is an intellectual belief. Giving him Lordship of your life implies following his leadership—learning his ways and walking in them.

A Christian is a Christ-follower or a disciple. Being a Christian is much like being a military service member in that it requires commitment, faith, and trust. Being a Christian means bearing Christ's name and surrendering to His leadership, sometimes at great personal cost. Our choice to become a service member is only for a short time, but our commitment to Christ lasts a lifetime and beyond.

Christianity is more than a religion.

It's a relationship with Christ.

If the idea of being a Christian is new to you, consider the following truths from the Bible:

- **John 14:6** *Jesus said to him, "I am the way, and the truth, and the life. No one comes to the Father except through me."*
- **John 3:16** *For God so loved the world, that he gave his only Son, that whoever believes in him should not perish but have eternal life.*

- **1 Peter 3:18** *For Christ also suffered once for sins, the righteous for the unrighteous, that he might bring us to God, being put to death in the flesh but made alive in the spirit.*
- **1 John 1:9** *If we confess our sins, he is faithful and just to forgive us our sins and to cleanse us from all unrighteousness.*

Are You Ready?

It simply takes a sincere prayer to be saved. If you need a little help, use the following prayer.

> *Lord Jesus, I know I have sinned against you. I come to you today with a repentant heart asking you to forgive my sin. I believe You are the Son of God. You came to earth and chose to die on the cross for me, and then rose again so that I could have eternal life. Beginning today, I surrender my life to you. In the holy name of Jesus, amen.*

If you prayed this prayer, please speak to your Bible study leader, a Christian friend, chaplain, or pastor. They can help you continue to learn more and grow in your walk with God.

Meet the Contributors

Author

Melissa Hicks is the author of *Flourish Wherever the Military Sends You*. She serves as the **Assistant Bible Study Coordinator** and **Staff Writer** for **Planting Roots**. She is a second-generation military brat who grew up on posts around the world. After college, she exchanged Army *brat* for Army *wife* and began a journey to help other military women grow in their faith.

Though she met Christ at an early age, Melissa continues to struggle with the difference between being a "good girl" and following Jesus. Thankfully, between the military and motherhood, God provides Melissa with ample proof of her own depravity, making the message of God's grace so much sweeter. A message so sweet, she desires to share it with others.

Melissa currently resides in Tampa, Florida, with her active duty husband, two sweet children, and a snuggly hound named Felix. In between PCS moves, she loves to write, spend time at the beach, and connect with friends new and old around the globe.

Content Contributors

Claudia Duff is a **Staff Writer.** As a member of the **Planting Roots** speaking team, she enjoys conducting workshops and speaking at their one-day events around the country. Claudia lives in Virginia with her retired Navy husband. Most days when she's not writing for **Planting Roots**, you can find her sitting in her sewing chair creating Grammy-made clothing for her GrandDufflings!

Muriel Gregory is a **Staff Writer** for **Planting Roots** who is a Christ follower, disciple maker, Bible Study teacher and lover of the Word. She is currently living in eastern Kansas and involved in a discipleship movement for the greater Kansas City area. Muriel and her active duty Army husband have been married twenty-four years. They have three children. Connect with Muriel on Instagram @Muriel.Gregory.

Jennifer Wake is the **Administration Team Lead** for **Planting Roots** and also serves on the writing team as a writer and administrative assistant. Jennifer has been a Christian for 30+ years and is still learning about Christ daily. As the wife of an Army chaplain, Jennifer has been involved in Protestant Women of the Chapel for eighteen years. Jennifer's true passion is to teach and to serve the military community.

Rachelle Whitfield is the **Marketing Team Lead** for **Planting Roots**. She is a veteran, Army wife and mom of four boys, two of whom have four paws. She has been a financial counselor in the military community for over ten years and a residential planner for nearly twenty years. She is passionate about helping military families create a lifestyle full of "ABUNDANCE." Connect with her on Instagram @rachellesamone.

Editors

Kristin Goodrich, known as "KG" on the **Planting Roots** team, serves as the **XO** (second in command) to the Director of **Planting Roots**. She proudly wore a Navy uniform for eight years and has been married to her retired Air Force husband for twenty-six years. She is third-generation Navy and is thankful for the opportunity to raise three kids in the military community. With a tendency to laugh loudly, KG loves to read lots of books, speak in various languages, do fire mitigation, and try new activities such as ballet. She is happy to have put down roots in Colorado.

Muriel Gregory is the **Bible Study Editor** for **Planting Roots**, a Christ follower, disciple maker, Bible Study teacher and lover of the Word. She is currently living in eastern Kansas and involved in a discipleship movement for the greater Kansas City area. Muriel and her active duty Army husband have been married twenty-four years. They have three children. Connect with Muriel on Instagram @Muriel.Gregory.

Ginger Harrington is the **Head of Publishing** and **Senior Editor** for **Planting Roots,** as well as serving on the **Speaking Team**. She is the author of the award-winning book, *Holy in the Moment: Simple Ways to Love God and Enjoy Your Life*. A blogger and engaging speaker for military and civilian audiences, Ginger writes at **www.GingerHarrington.com**. Ginger has also edited, formatted, and compiled *Free to Be Brave: Moments with God for Military Life* and edited *Beyond Brave: Faith to Stand in Military Life*. Ginger and her retired Marine husband have been married for twenty-eight years and have three young adult children. Visit Ginger's website or connect with her on Facebook or Instagram @*GingerHarrington*.

Andrea Plotner serves as an **Editor** for **Planting Roots**. She is author of *Beyond Brave*, a six-week Bible study published by Planting Roots. Andrea and her family live and work at Spring Canyon, a Christ-centered conference center ministering to military families in the Colorado Rockies. Andrea is a motivator, encouraging women to get "into" God's Word. For fun Andrea teaches Pilates, reads voraciously, and keeps an eye out for everyday adventure.

Chaplain, Major General Cecil R. Richardson, U.S. Air Force, Retired serves on the **Board of Directors** for **Planting Roots.** Chaplain Cecil Richardson served 41½ years in the military, retiring as the Chief of Chaplains, He retired in 2012 as the Chief of Chaplains, Chairman of the Armed Forced Chaplains Board, and Advisor to the Secretary of Defense and the Joint Chiefs of Staff on religious, ethical, and quality-of-life concerns. Chaplain Richardson and his wife, Dr. Jan Richardson, an author and literacy consultant, have three sons: Steve, an Air Force chaplain (lieutenant colonel); Jim, Assistant Secretary of State, Foreign Aid; and Mike, Chief Electrical Engineer, Los Alamos Nuclear Laboratories.

About Planting Roots

They will be like a tree planted by the water that sends out its roots by the stream. It does not fear when heat comes; its leaves are always green. It has not worries in a year of drought and never fails to bear fruit.
—Jeremiah 17:8

Planting Roots is a 501c3 not-for-profit organization created by military women for military women. Our goal is to empower military women to fulfill God's purpose wherever they are planted, for however long they are there. Whether we are women in uniform, military wives, female veterans, or other women connected to the military, we all experience the joys and challenges of military life. We desire to build connections by planting roots of faith and friendship that provide strength to thrive in military life.

Planting Roots encourages and equips women to plant their roots deep in Jesus Christ through biblically-based resources, live events, and online community. Cultivating a deeper walk with Christ and investing in our community, **Planting Roots** empowers Christian military women to become stronger together. Technology allows us to cultivate a global community of like-minded, faith-filled women on a mission wherever the military sends us. As Christian military women, we seek to impact our communities by doing the work God has called us to do, in the places we are planted. Together, we impact the world for Christ.

Please join our online community at www.PlantingRoots.net. Register your email address through our website to receive inspiration in your inbox, and be sure to follow us on social media for new resources. **Find us on Facebook @MilitaryWivesandWomen; on Instagram @PlantingRoots; and on Twitter @PlantingRoots1.**

We look forward to meeting you at our next live event! You can find our conference schedule on our website. By subscribing to our emails, you'll know as soon as new events are announced!

Please consider how you may participate in the ministry of **Planting Roots**. Feel free to submit a guest post to our blog at **www.PlantingRoots.net/writers-guidelines/** or check out the tab "Join Us' to find out more about praying with and for us, supporting **Planting Roots** financially, or seeing what volunteer job positions are open at this time. Every gift is carefully stewarded in order to maximize each dollar and to support military women worldwide.

Join us on our website!

Sunday Prayer

Join us in praying for our nation and the men, women, and families who serve in the military.

Monday Minute

Sharing stories of how we grow in faith in military life.

Worship Wednesday

Draw close to Jesus with inspiration to ignite worship in the midst of military life.

Be a Guest Writer

Submission guidelines available on our website!

BEYOND BRAVE: FAITH TO STAND FIRM IN MILITARY LIFE
A Six-Week Study of Galatians 5

Enjoy *Beyond Brave: Faith to Stand Firm in Military Life,* a six-week Bible study on Galatians 5 and a companion study for the devotional *Free to be Brave.* Dig into the freeing truths in this key chapter in the Bible. In the military, we understand the fight for freedom from a unique perspective. As women in uniform or women in military families, we understand the snares and pitfalls that pervade our daily lives—stress, worry, insecurity, and self-sufficiency vs. God-dependency. With lessons and examples applied to military life, Beyond Brave will show you how to stand firm on God's truth, even in the challenges of military experience. Go beyond the battles you face today and be brave in the good fight of faith. Available at Amazon.

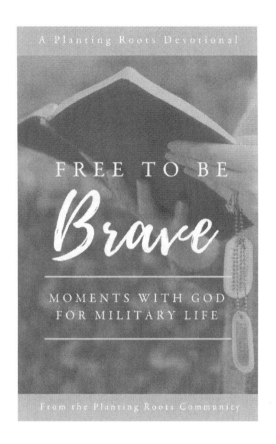

FREE TO BE BRAVE: MOMENTS WITH GOD FOR MILITARY LIFE
A Planting Roots Devotional

Whether you are a uniformed woman or a female family member, military life can be challenging. Written by military women for military women, *Free to Be Brave* offers moments with God for military life. Remember God's promise of freedom from weariness, fear, conflict and guilt. Discover the blessings of living in Christ's freedom to be brave, authentic, grateful, and hopeful. A companion devotional for the study *Beyond Brave*, both books are written by the *Planting Roots* writing team. Join the women from the *Planting Roots* community and thrive in military life! Available at Amazon.

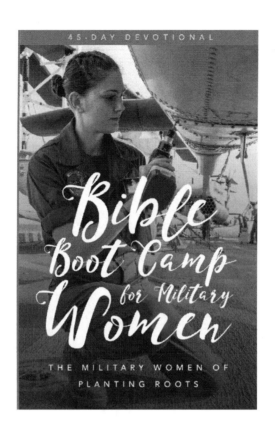

BIBLE BOOT CAMP FOR MILITARY WOMEN
A 45-Day Devotional

New to the Bible or Bible study? Hoping for a user-friendly look at God's story from beginning to end? Written by the *Planting Roots* team, *Bible Boot Camp* will help you understand the Bible. Designed specifically for women in uniform, each lesson is short and to the point. The personal stories tucked into these pages show faith-forward examples from the lives of women in uniform, as well as military wives, family members, and retirees. Published in partnership with the **American Bible Society**, *Bible Boot Camp for Military Women* is a free resource. Contact your local military chaplain for ordering copies of this and other free resources from the **American Bible Society** (americanbible.org).

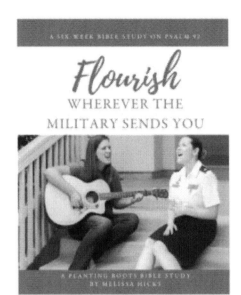

Flourish Wherever the Military Sends You
A Six-Week Bible Study on Psalm 92

Bloom where you're planted. Great advice. But what does that even mean? What does the Bible say about flourishing?

Based on solid principles from the word of God, this study of Psalm 92 will teach you:

- How to show gratitude when all you want to do is complain
- How to praise God for who he is, not just what he does
- How to spend time in God's presence even when life is hard
- How to love others when military life stresses you out and wears you down

Join us on a journey through Psalm 92, and begin to live the flourishing life Jesus promised. Available at Amazon.

Made in the USA
Columbia, SC
31 March 2022

58363720R00093